Trading in Commodities
An Investors Chronicle Guide

GW01057564

Trading in Commodities

An Investors Chronicle Guide

Editor:

C. W. J. GRANGER, B.A., Ph.D.

*Professor of Applied Statistics and Econometrics,
University of Nottingham*

WOODHEAD-FAULKNER : CAMBRIDGE

Woodhead-Faulkner Ltd,
7 Rose Crescent,
Cambridge CB2 3LL

First published March 1974

ISBN 0 85941 008 0

Printed in Great Britain by Galliard (Printers) Limited,
Great Yarmouth, Norfolk

Foreword

F. F. WOLFF
Chairman, The Federation of Commodity Associations

The publishers of this book have performed a useful service in providing a volume of medium size which gives a good description of the methods of trading in commodities together with a glossary of terms which will help the reader to understand how the commodity markets, exchanges and auctions function. In all trades there are skills and techniques to be mastered, and, frequently, a vocabulary of technical terms or jargon. The commodity trades have their fair share!

The Federation of Commodity Associations is constantly receiving requests for information about commodities from many different sources which include business firms, both at home and abroad, financial institutions, potential investors, professional writers and students. There is a wealth of information in this book for all of them.

Acknowledgements

The Editor and publishers wish to express their gratitude to all those individuals, companies and associations who have given assistance during the preparation of this book and are particularly indebted to the following: Mr R. C. Hughes, Director, The Federation of Commodity Associations; Mr J. H. Farr, Secretary, The Federation of Commodity Associations; Mr M. Stockdale, Director, The International Commodities Clearing House Ltd; Mr N. J. Ferrier, Business Development Executive, The International Commodities Clearing House Ltd; Mr P. A. S. Rucker, Secretary, The London Commodity Exchange; Mr J. L. Bailey, Secretary, The Rubber Trade Association of London; Mr A. A. Hooker, Managing Director, A. A. Hooker & Co. Ltd (for permission to include material originally published in his book *The London "Home Grown" Grain Futures Markets*); Mr B. D. G. Antrobus, Rudolf Wolff & Co. Ltd; Mr C. C. Coombs; Reuters Economic Services Ltd; Moodies Services Ltd; Wallace Brothers Commodities Ltd; Jeremy Oates Ltd; Commodity Management Services Ltd; Commodity Analysis Ltd; Chart Analysis Ltd (for permission to reproduce the point and figure chart in Chapter 7); Investment Research (for permission to reproduce all other illustrations in Chapter 7 and the charts of spot prices in Chapters 4 and 5).

Contents

Notes on Editor and Contributors

C. W. J. Granger is Professor of Applied Statistics and Econometrics at the University of Nottingham but in late 1974 will take up a position as Professor of Economics at the University of California, San Diego. He has spent most of his career at Nottingham, where he obtained a first-class honours degree in Mathematics in 1955 and a Ph.D. in Statistics in 1959. After a year at Princeton University he was appointed Lecturer at Nottingham and later Reader and then Professor, in the departments of Mathematics and Economics. He has also taught at Stanford University, in Vienna and elsewhere. His main research interests are in statistical forecasting, speculative markets and consumer price attitudes, and these studies have led to the publication of three books, including *Speculation, Hedging and Commodity Price Forecasts*, of which he is co-author, and over fifty articles.

L. A. Brighton commenced his career in commodities in London immediately after the Second World War with a well-known cocoa and general produce broker. He graduated from the shipping documentation department and within a year or so was marketing all kinds of produce—spices, fibres, cocoa, coffee, sugar, etc. At this time the world markets were opening up again after long closures and this afforded him experience so that when Merrill Lynch, the world's largest commission house, decided to have an agent in London his firm was selected. Within a short time Merrill Lynch opened their own London office and he was appointed their first commodity trader. Under his guidance and encouragement the office expanded from a four-man concern in late 1960 to become the largest commodity operation of its kind in London.

P. J. Cornish is the Managing Director of Commodity Management Services and has been involved in the commodity markets for the majority of his working life. In 1970 CMS became a wholly owned subsidiary of Ralli Trading Finance Ltd (of which Mr Cornish is also a director), a company in the Bowater Ralli Group. CMS specialises particularly in handling discretionary accounts for the private and institutional investor both in the United Kingdom and abroad, and, in addition to its London operation, has a Swiss office based in Geneva.

M. E. T. Davies is Joint Managing Director of Inter Commodities Ltd, a company specialising in handling private and institutional investment on the world's commodity markets. He started his career with the Ralli International Group, where he gained a wide experience in all the major commodities. In conjunction with his present co-directors, he then founded Inter Commodities, which has now been built up into one of the most respected companies of its type. He is a frequent contributor to several of the United Kingdom's leading financial journals.

T. S. E. Figgis joined his family business, S. Figgis & Co. Ltd, founded in 1890 by his grandfather, in October 1923. Apart from six years in the Army during the Second World War, he has spent the whole of his working life in commodities. Three times President of the General Produce Brokers Association of London (in 1939, 1947 and 1955), he was Chairman of the Rubber Trade Association of London in 1969 and still serves on its committees.

R. Gibson-Jarvie was educated at Rugby and Trinity Hall, Cambridge, where he obtained a B.A.(Hons.) in Law. He is a member of the Bar and served throughout the Second World War in the Royal Navy. His business career commenced at United Dominions Trust, of which his father, the late J. Gibson-Jarvie, was founder and then Chairman. When UDT took over the shares in the London Produce Clearing House (now the International Commodities Clearing House) in 1950, he was appointed to the board of that company. Thus began his connection with the commodity markets which has continued—after a break of some years in the late 1960s—through his appointment with the London Metal Exchange in the latter part of 1970. He represents the LME on the Council of the Federation of Commodity Associations.

P. Lynch-Garbett, after his wartime military service, first entered the commodity world in 1947 in London and in 1948 was assigned to Sydney, where during the next five years he was involved commercially in the marketing of wool. In 1953 he returned to the United Kingdom for the inauguration of a new London wool futures market (London Wool Terminal Market Association) and from then on took an active part in the development of futures. Having spent a number of years on the Management Committee of the LWTMA, he was elected to Chairman in

1970. In 1959 he joined Bache & Co. (London) Ltd, a wholly owned subsidiary of the international brokerage house, Bache & Co. Inc., and was soon elected to the London board. In 1968 he was appointed an officer of the parent company. In recent years, as Sales Director of Bache & Co. (London) Ltd, his responsibilities have embraced the servicing and promotion of commodity futures business both in the United Kingdom and internationally.

T. H. Stewart was educated at Westminster School and Trinity College, Cambridge, where he obtained a degree in History. Upon graduating, he remained in Cambridge to join Investment Research, where he has been ever since and in which he is now a partner. Since 1967 he has been responsible for the commodities publication side of the firm which produces the weekly London Commodity Charts Service.

Chapter 1

An Introduction to Investments: Return and Risk

C. W. J. GRANGER

THE VARIETY OF AVAILABLE INVESTMENTS

An investor, either an individual or an institution, faces a great variety of possible investments in which to place any spare cash that is not immediately required to meet day-to-day living expenses. These possible investments include the Post Office Savings Bank, a bank deposit account, Premium Bonds and Government Bonds, the shares and bonds of a great diversity of companies, investment trusts of many types and aspirations, land, pictures, stamps—and commodities. Each type of investment has its own unique features representing both advantages and disadvantages, and by combining different types of investment, that is forming a "portfolio" of investments, the needs and requirements of virtually any investor can be satisfied.

Nevertheless, to decide upon his personal portfolio, the investor needs to appreciate the properties of the available investments. While most can fully understand how to invest in the Post Office Savings Bank or in shares, many do not appreciate the benefits, and problems, that can arise from putting money into commodities. It is hoped that this book will help to dispel the sense of mystery that many potential investors feel surrounds the commodity markets. It is certainly true that the markets do contain a plentiful supply of weird technical terms, such as backwardation and contango, but what sophisticated field of human endeavour does not? All the important terms will be explained in the text, and a glossary is also provided at the end of the book. Some may also find the notion of trading in futures rather than in physical entities to be odd when first encountered, but when one becomes used to the idea it will soon be appreciated that futures trading possesses an intriguing degree of flexibility and subtlety that makes for particularly interesting investment possibilities. This is especially true for the person who wants to feel completely and continuously involved with his investment.

Investments can vary in three basic ways—in their degree of liquidity,

1

in the return that one can expect and in the level of risk inherent in the investment. An investment is said to be liquid if one can convert it into cash almost immediately whenever one wishes and it is generally assumed that private investors prefer to hold at least part of their savings in such assets. Examples of liquid assets are shares and Premium Bonds. However, some assets are not liquid; for example there are restrictions on the amounts one can draw immediately from a Post Office Savings account or from a deposit account in most banks. Some types of life insurance are very non-liquid, as one cannot get at the deposits until an agreed number of years have passed. An investment in a physical good such as a stamp, a picture or some property is not necessarily very liquid, as one cannot always find a willing buyer at exactly the right moment. The ability to sell such investments with little delay is known as the marketability of the good. Investments such as shares in most large companies are liquid only because there are so many "players" in the market that they are easily marketed, or traded, but a large holding in a minor company may well be difficult to sell at any given moment. The same is true of commodities: most are easily marketed, but some are not so at all times. Thus, if one is particularly concerned with liquidity, it is better to stick to the more popular commodities.

Consideration of return and risk will be taken up in a later section of this chapter, after commodity markets themselves have been briefly introduced.

COMMODITY MARKETS: AN OVERVIEW OF THE BOOK

A commodity market was originally merely a place where commodity producers could meet with users of the commodity and, via an auction, reach a current selling price. However, as will be explained in the following chapter, the need for futures selling became obvious so that the producers and users and also various other traders, particularly middlemen, could reduce the risks and uncertainty that arose from the natural fluctuations in prices. A "buy" futures contract is an intention to buy a set quantity at a previously agreed price at a certain time in the future, known as the terminal date or month. Such a contract can be completely cancelled out by later taking up a "sell" futures contract for the same trading position. Thus, the investor in futures need not be involved in actual physical trading of the commodity, but almost inevitably trades only in these intentions, or futures.

There are thus three viewpoints that can be taken of a commodity market—that of a typical investor, that of a producer and that of a businessman who has to buy his raw materials on the market. The contents of this book are aimed at the first and third of these groups.

In Chapter 2, an account is given of the origin and current operating mechanism of the markets, together with a description of how futures contracts are used and how businessmen's risks can be reduced by hedging. Chapter 3 considers the types of trading used on futures markets in further detail.

The following two chapters then consider the various features of the London markets and include specific suggestions about how to trade effectively in these markets. Chapter 4 deals with the soft commodities, such as sugar, cocoa, coffee and grains, and Chapter 5 considers rubber, metals and bullion.

The second half of the book tries to give practical advice to traders about what strategies to use and where to obtain relevant information and help. Chapter 6 is aimed primarily at the private investor or speculator and Chapter 8 at the businessman. In Chapter 7, the critically important problem of how to forecast prices is considered from various viewpoints and advice is given on how to use various kinds of price charts. Finally, Chapter 9 outlines where publicly available information can be obtained, and the book ends with a short glossary and a summary of the main features of the London markets.

The advice given should be quite sufficient for an investor to be able to make his initial venture into the market with a reasonable likelihood of achieving a success. The level of sophistication that can be applied to one's strategy in the market is almost limitless, but it has yet to be proved that such sophistication necessarily pays off in terms of profits. The book does not attempt to discuss complicated strategies but rather to provide clear, simple and worthwhile advice.

An investor entering the commodity markets for the first time will find a much more exciting type of investment than most others available to him. Prices can fluctuate quickly and so returns can be high, but so also will be risks. As it is important to appreciate this risk aspect, it is discussed in some detail in the following section. This chapter ends with a brief comparison of features of the stock and commodity markets: there are considerable differences between them, and they need to be understood by investors already familiar with the former market. It is these differences that recommend commodity markets to an increasing number of investors as a place to put at least part of their available liquid assets to work.

RETURN AND RISK

The return on an investment is usually taken to be the gain (or loss) over some stated period measured as a percentage of the capital involved, *i.e.*

$$\text{Return} = \frac{\text{Final value} - \text{Initial value of investment}}{\text{Initial value}} \times 100$$

It is natural to prefer an investment that gives a high return to one with a low return, but unfortunately comparison of investments is complicated by the fact that there is also a second dimension, the level of risk.

Risk is much more difficult to measure and partly depends on the attitudes of the individual. To some, an investment may seem risky if it cannot be converted immediately into cash at all times, so that a very specialised antique which is not necessarily readily sold would appear risky. However, to most, risk can be related to the possibility of getting an unsatisfactory return such as a negative return, or loss. It is clear that risk arises because of uncertainty about what will occur in the future, but there is not an exact relationship between risk and uncertainty. Suppose one is given a bond and told that almost certainly one will get a return of 10 per cent but that there is a possibility of getting 20 per cent. As either return is acceptable, the uncertainty in the return one will get cannot be associated with risk, as risk is inherently unpleasant.

As an example of a risky asset, suppose one is told that the odds of getting a 10 per cent return are 3 to 5 and that the odds of getting a return of minus 10 per cent, that is a loss, are 2 to 5. Although one will get a reasonable return *on average*, as a positive return is more likely to occur than a negative one, nevertheless one may well end up with a loss and so risk is involved.

Most investments involve some risk. For example, a fixed-interest asset, such as a bank deposit account, gives a certain return and may thus seem riskless, but in a period of inflation if the return is measured in terms of what one can buy with one's cash—that is, the real value rather than the monetary value—then the actual return could be negative. A Premium Bond, if one does not win, is effectively giving one a negative return, as the actual return is zero, and one has also lost the opportunity of getting a positive return from a fixed-interest investment, this being called the opportunity cost of the investment. A share is obviously a risky asset, as it is very possible to get a negative return over any prescribed period.

Most investors are risk-averse, in the sense that if offered two investments with the same return most would choose the one that was less risky. However, in practice one has to balance one's desire for a high return against a reluctance to undertake high risk. This arises because it is generally believed, and is well supported by empirical evidence, that assets with high returns are typically also those with high levels of risk, those with the lowest returns generally having low risk. There is not a perfect relationship between risk and return but the rule is worth remembering when investing. A pair of investments that do not obey the rule are leaving one's money in a tin box under the bed (zero return, risk of being stolen not negligible) compared to cash put into a Post Office Savings account (fixed return, only risk arising from uncertain level of inflation). For this pair, the second is said to dominate the first, having both a higher return and a lower risk.

A sensible way of reducing risk is to spread one's investments over several assets, rather than putting all of one's eggs in one basket. The best way to build up a portfolio is a very complicated procedure that is attempted by very few investors, but a good rule is to put part of one's savings into a fixed-interest, low-risk asset and to spread the rest over three or four assets, such as shares, investment trust bonds and commodities, whose prices do not move closely together.

A proposal originally made by academics, but now accepted by many investment analysts and professional investors, is that an asset whose price fluctuates a great deal is riskier than one whose price does not. That this is sensible can be seen by noting that, if the price changes a lot, then over some set period a rather large negative return can result, particularly if one buys at a high and sells at a low. It may be thought that this problem can be overcome by choosing the most opportune time at which to sell, but this could result in one's capital being tied up in a low-return asset for long periods. To take an extreme example, if one had bought at the 1929 high in US shares, one could not have sold at a higher price until the early 1950s. Taking this view of risk, commodities are a highly risky asset, as prices are inclined to move faster and over larger ranges than most share prices, for example. However, as returns can also be very large, it is clearly sensible to consider making commodities part of one's portfolio so as to have the chance of making a good overall return.

Because of the high risk levels associated with commodities, a person who plays the market is perhaps better called a speculator rather than an investor. Although a speculator is involved with risk, he should not be equated with a gambler, as his trading strategy can be designed to limit the risks he takes. How this can be done will be discussed in Chapters 2, 3 and 6.

COMPARISON OF STOCK AND COMMODITY MARKETS

Although similarities can be found between stock and commodity markets, they are basically quite different and one has to take a very different attitude towards them when forecasting prices or contemplating an investment policy. On the stock market, the trading is almost exclusively in shares that were issued in previous years, possibly ones that were issued a very long time ago. Very few of the trades involve new shares, either new issues by established companies or the shares of new companies "going public". In fact, British industry raises very little of its new investment capital on the stock market, perhaps only around 10 per cent. However, to the companies issuing new shares, this is an important source of capital and it would be very unlikely that they would be able to sell their shares if there did not exist such an active stock market, thereby making the level of marketability of the new shares an acceptable one.

The commodity market is much nearer to the "pure market" so beloved by classical economists, in which goods are brought by the producers and purchased by intending users at a price determined by current demand and supply. The fact that much of the trading on commodity markets is done by speculators dilutes this picture, but nevertheless real goods either recently produced or about to be produced are traded and make up the principal raw materials in many important manufacturing processes. The commodity market thus seems to be more nearly a "real" market than does a stock exchange on which the same pieces of paper are merely exchanged around. On the commodity markets the presence of speculators acts as a lubricant, increasing marketability and thereby making the markets more useful to the producers and users. However, commodity markets do not have anything equivalent to dividends, which generally sweeten the holding of shares.

A basic difference is that virtually everyone holding shares benefits if prices rise and loses if prices fall. It is only the lack of sufficient mutual confidence that prevents stock prices rising continuously. On commodity markets, some speculators will go "short" and others "long"; that is, some will bet on prices falling and others hope that prices will rise. Similarly, producers of the commodity would prefer high prices whereas users of the commodity clearly prefer low prices. There are thus two sides to any commodity market, pushing in opposite directions. This could partly explain why commodity prices are sometimes more unstable, or dynamic, than stock prices.

Prices are reached on a commodity market by an almost pure auction, whereas this is much less so on a stock exchange, owing to the operations of jobbers, who are known as specialists in the New York exchanges.

A further very basic difference is the size of margins, or deposits, required. On the stock market, or if one actually buys a physical quantity of a commodity, one has to pay almost the full price in cash, but on the commodity futures market one can operate on a deposit of only around 10 per cent. At one time lower deposits were available on some stock exchanges but it was found that the extra degree of risk introduced into transactions could not justify low deposits. On a futures market such considerations are of less importance and the existence of low deposits means that one can contemplate large returns with less of one's capital tied up. Similarly, one's losses can be greater, measured as a percentage of capital employed.

There is also an important difference between the investor's horizons in the two markets. On the stock market, one buys a share and can hold on to it for as long as one wishes. It is always possible just to forget about the share for several years. This would not be possible with a futures contract, which has a fixed and predetermined terminal date or month, before which a counteracting futures contract has to be entered into. This could be arranged to occur automatically by instructing one's broker accordingly, but nevertheless one will be back to holding cash again within a fixed period. Thus, the investor on the commodity futures market is necessarily more involved with his investments than need be a shareholder.

Concerning risks, the commodity markets are generally accepted to be the more risky of the two, especially as it is possible to diversify one's investment in shares by putting money into an investment trust, or mutual fund in the United States, whereas similar institutions are less well developed for commodity markets. There is evidence that price changes on the commodity markets are not affected by stock market price changes and vice versa. It thus follows that an investment spread between the two markets in the appropriate ratio will be less risky than either, and probably will give a higher return than an investment just in shares.

Perhaps the main similarities between the markets are that the private investor has to approach both through specialist brokers and that prices on both are notoriously difficult to forecast, so difficult in fact that some investigators believe that it is virtually impossible to forecast price changes—an idea which academics call the "random walk hypothesis". However, a different viewpoint is taken in Chapter 7.

Chapter 2

The Purpose and Workings of Commodity Markets

C. W. J. GRANGER

WHY COMMODITY MARKETS?

The economy of nations, and hence of the world, depends heavily on the act of trading. There may be numerous reasons why it is more economical to produce some good at one place rather than another, including physical, climatological, social and political reasons. The movement of these goods from their original source in response to some consumer demand will raise their value. For example, a plough just leaving a factory in Manchester has one value, a fairly low one in fact as the opportunities for ploughing in Manchester are fairly limited, but if transported to a cotton field in the Sudan it has much greater value. Similarly, a field of cotton in the Sudan has little immediate value to the farmer, as he cannot eat it, but if taken to a mill in Manchester the value of the cotton increases greatly, as it can be transformed into manufactured cotton goods both of direct value to Mancunians and for further trading. This simple example exhibits most of the important elements in commodity trading: transport, storage through time and the differing values placed on the commodity by buyers and sellers.

As some commodities, such as coffee beans, can be produced in various countries and will be required by manufacturers in many other countries, it is clearly beneficial for the traders to meet regularly in just a few trading centres rather than having representatives travelling haphazardly around the world. These centres are the commodity markets and they exist for a wide range of commodities: grains, edible oils and fats, cotton, coffee, cocoa, metals and so forth. It should be clear that the necessity for such a market arises only when both buyers and sellers are numerous. Thus one would not expect, or get, a market for new Rover cars or any other branded good, as there is only one manufacturer. The reason for having a branded good is to try to induce some unique features about one's manufactures and so possibly reduce the extent to which it is substitutable for a similar good produced by another manufacturer. This would not be true of copper ore, for example, as the ore produced in one country is almost perfectly substitutable for that produced in another, even though they may have slightly different chemical properties. The commodities with which we shall be concerned will all be unbranded and generally will have been either mined or grown.

If there are many buyers and sellers in the market place, it is natural for some kind of auction to take place, and the sales that take place will determine the current price of the commodity. However, in practice, there are not always dozens of sellers and hundreds of buyers in the market on every day: there may, for example, be effectively only four or five large cocoa producers and a score or so of large manufacturers who want to buy this commodity. If the markets were organised in the simple way outlined above, it would be very possible that a potential buyer could go to the market on some occasion but not find a seller. In other words, the degree of marketability of the product would be low. This problem is reduced by the fact that commodity markets are open to anyone to trade. An "investor"—although "speculator" may be a better term—can enter the market, buy some of the commodity and hold it, hoping that the price will rise, so that he can eventually sell at a profit. The presence of such investors in the market place will help make it a continuous market, so that a price for the commodity is always available. The price at which one can currently buy a commodity is known as the "spot" or cash price. The obvious difficulty with a commodity is that there are various holding costs. If spot markets were the only ones that existed, there would be little interest in them for the majority of investors, but in fact the commodity markets have developed in such a way that they are much more attractive to speculators.

THE FORWARD CONTRACT

The first stage of this development was the availability of forward contracts. A manufacturer, knowing that he will require a certain quantity of a commodity in, say, six months' time, will try to find a seller who will guarantee to supply this quantity at the stated time and at a price mutually agreed between them at the time the contract is made. Thus, for example, a maker of chocolates will contract to buy 100 tons of cocoa from a grower at £500 a ton, the cocoa to be delivered in six months' time. At the time the contract is made, the cocoa may still be ripening on the trees, but, nevertheless, the contract is a firm commitment on both parties.

There is an obvious advantage to both parties from making such a contract. The buyer may know that he can make an adequate profit if he can buy his main raw material at £500 a ton and the grower may feel that he is also getting a worthwhile return at this price. Thus, both have saved themselves the uncertainty, or risk, of selling or buying at whatever turns out to be the spot price in six months' time. If, in fact, the spot price does go up over the six months, the buyer particularly will have benefited from the contract, but, if the spot price falls over the period, the seller will have benefited most. However, as neither will know for certain which way prices will move, both are likely to be willing to forgo any windfall gain by removing the possibility of any equivalent loss.

The price at which the forward contract is made need not be the same as the current spot price. It may be generally agreed, for example, that spot prices are more likely to increase than to decrease in the immediate future, and so a forward price somewhat above the current spot price would be appropriate, although the difference in price could not be more than the cost to the buyer of buying at the current spot price and then paying storage costs over the next few months. (When forward prices are greater than current spot prices, one is in a "contango situation", in the terminology of the market.) Similarly, if prices are thought more likely to fall than increase, the forward contract price may be lower than the current spot price (known as a "backwardation").

Once made available on the commodity exchanges in the last century, the forward contracts quickly became very popular as manufacturers found they could order their supplies from origin and could therefore manage with much lower levels of stocks. Thus, auctioning of commodity lots that had reached the dockside was largely replaced by what is still known as c.i.f. trading, meaning that the price paid by the purchaser covers cost, insurance and freight. The transaction was thus agreed upon by the buyer and seller before the produce was shipped from its country of origin, resulting not only in worthwhile reductions in warehousing and handling charges but also in a reduction in the uncertainty referred to before.

The development of the large-scale use of forward contracts depended heavily on a reliable system of grading of commodities as well as the growth of speedy and reliable systems of communication and shipping, such as the organisation of a worldwide postal system, the opening of the Suez Canal and the invention of the telegraph.

Although the forward contract was a clear improvement over the spot contract, and is still widely used, it nevertheless still had some disadvantages. It was rather inflexible, being a fixed contract between two parties that could not easily be rearranged so that a third party took over part of the contract. Thus, if the sugar crop of a particular grower was badly hit by a hurricane, he could not easily pass on his part of the contract to a grower with plenty of sugar. Further, to arrange such a contract, a buyer and a seller both had to be in the market at the same time and with similar horizons and price expectations. Putting it in another way, the market was sometimes "thin", with an insufficient number of either buyers or sellers present on some occasions. Thus, a manufacturer might have found that he could not arrange a suitable forward contract at the precise moment that he wanted. To overcome these difficulties, a contract that was both more flexible and more sophisticated was developed, known as the futures contract. It was this contract that attracted speculators to the market—in fact it is necessary for speculators to take an interest in such contracts for the futures market to work efficiently.

FUTURES MARKETS

The forward contract was concerned with a specific item of produce and was binding on both parties. The contract that evolved from it, known as the futures contract, is merely a promise to deliver a commodity of a stated grade. When this new contract appeared traders were no longer limited by the number of contracts available at any one time on the forward market but were free to draw up obligations according to need. It further followed that the market was greatly increased in size owing to the scope given to speculators to participate in the market by originating contracts themselves.

A futures contract works as follows: suppose that on 1 January an investor considers the change in price of, say, coffee between that date and nine months hence, on 30 September. Suppose further that he is offered a certain quantity of the commodity at £X per unit to be delivered on 30 September, the terminal date. If he believes that the spot price of coffee will be greater than £X on 30 September he will agree to this contract and, clearly, if his expectation is correct he will make a profit by taking delivery of the commodity on the terminal date and then selling immediately on the spot market. However, if on 1 March, say, he finds another investor who is willing to pay £Y per unit, where Y is greater than X, for coffee to be delivered on 30 September, then the owner of the contract may decide to take an immediate profit, particularly if he doubts whether the spot price will be above £Y on the terminal date. He therefore agrees to a sell futures contract at £Y per unit on 1 March for the specified quantity of coffee with 30 September as the terminal date. When the terminal date eventually arrives, his own buy and sell contracts will cancel out and he will not be involved in the eventual settlement. In fact, most speculators would expect to take out such a cancelling contract well before the settlement date, either to take a profit if prices have moved favourably for them or to limit their loss if prices have gone the other way. If one buys a futures contract with the intention of later cancelling it out by a corresponding sale, so that one hopes for an increase in prices, one is said to hold a "long position".

If one expects prices to fall, the reverse position is taken. On 1 January the investor agrees to sell coffee on 30 September at £X per unit and he will usually then cancel this by agreeing at a later date to a buy futures contract for the same quantity and the same terminal date. As he is hoping for a price fall, then on 1 January he is said to hold a "short position", as he has sold on the futures market and expects to cancel this by buying later. At first sight it may seem strange to agree to sell something that one does not possess, but this is explained by the fact that one intends to buy the commodity or its equivalent at a later date. If the trader does allow this sell futures contract to exist through to the terminal date, then he will have to buy on the spot market to meet this commitment. However, in the majority of cases a speculator will not hold his contract this long and generally buys a matching, and cancelling, contract at some earlier date. It has been estimated that in the order of 90 per cent of all futures contracts do not run to settlement—that is, only about 10 per cent are not matched with a contract in the other direction.

As a simple example, suppose a speculator buys on 10 January 1974 100 tons of August sugar at £120 a ton, so that he takes a long position. The commodity he buys is called August sugar because August is the terminal month of the contract. If then he sells on 6 March 1974 August sugar at £145 a ton, his balance sheet will be:

		£
10.1.74	Buy 100 tons August sugar at £120 a ton:	12,000
6.3.74	Sell 100 tons August sugar at £145 a ton:	14,500
	Gross profit	2,500
	Commission	18
	Net profit	2,482

Here, the broker's commission has been taken to be £9 per contract of 50 tons, this being a turn-round rate, inclusive of the exchange's clearing fee. As an example of a short position, consider this pair of futures contracts:

		£
4.3.74	Sell 10 long tons November coffee at £450 a ton:	4,500
10.7.74	Buy 10 long tons November coffee at £470 a ton:	4,700
	Gross loss	200
	Commission	14
	Net loss	214

Thus in this example the short position has not paid off and, to get out of the contract before even greater losses occur, it has been cancelled with a buy contract. The example also illustrates the fact that losses can happen. It is interesting to note that most of the brochures on commodity markets issued by those who specialise in attracting speculators, although mentioning the possibility of losses, always include specific examples in which the speculator has made a handsome profit. Specific marketing details such as the size of commissions and the minimum contract sizes are given for the major commodities traded in London in Appendix 2.

One aspect of the above sums that is particularly important to the average investor is that all futures are conducted on a margin of around 10 to 20 per cent. Thus, in the first example, to buy the 100 tons of sugar, at a total value of £12,000, the investor has to lay out only around £1200 to £2400. This means that the profit on this deal, measured as a percentage of the capital involved, is quite tremendous. On the other hand, a loss could completely wipe out one's capital. If prices change sufficiently against the original contract the broker will ask for a further margin by the investor.

It must be noted that the investor is keeping his eyes on a fixed date in the future, the terminal date, and that he has to make a series of decisions about when to buy or sell as time passes and the interval until the arrival of the terminal date decreases. The existence of the "deadline" imposed by the terminal date makes investing in commodities rather different to other types of investment, where one's horizons can be more flexible. It should also be clear that there is a strong tendency for futures with a fixed terminal date and spot prices to move towards each other as the terminal date approaches the present. This must occur if futures are above spot, as if, for example, July cocoa futures in June were substantially higher than the present spot price, it would pay to sell July cocoa and buy cocoa on the spot market, store the cocoa for a month and then settle the futures contract with the stored commodity. Such a policy is only occasionally possible but is inevitably profitable provided futures are above spot by a sufficient amount to cover storage costs and commissions. Apart from this effect, spot prices and futures prices for sufficiently distant terminal dates can be quite different. There is, nevertheless, a general tendency for spot and futures prices to move together, although this cannot always be relied upon.

Further advice and details of trading on futures markets, which are also called terminal markets, can be found in Chapters 3 and 6. The number of terminal dates or months varies from one market to another, but they can extend as much as two and a half years into the future.

BUSINESSMEN AND THE FUTURES MARKETS

We have just considered the futures market from the viewpoint of a speculator but, contrary to the attitude of many popular writers, these markets do not exist for the exclusive benefit of speculators, but rather to provide a market for businessmen, that is middlemen, commodity producers and commodity users. No single group is of paramount importance and the markets could not exist in their present form without any one of these main groups. A commodity producer can use the futures market just like a forward contract. By selling a futures contract he ensures a set price for his produce for some specific time into the future, thus removing the risks involved in selling on a market with unstable prices. The only immediate difference for the producer is that he will not know to whom his produce will be delivered until the eventual settling-up is conducted by the exchange, as described below. However, the futures contract does have further advantages to the producer, as, if his crop or level of production does not live up to expectations, he can make up the difference by buying on the futures market, although possibly at a loss, if there is general realisation of a potential shortage of the commodity. This is one reason why producers frequently take great pains to keep secret the quality or size of a crop or the level of production of a mineral.

Similarly, an industrial manufacturer can ensure a continual supply of his basic raw materials at a relatively constant price by buying the necessary futures contracts. Again, the removal of risk, or uncertainty, allows him to plan his future production efficiently. A manufacturer of chocolate, for instance, faces quite enough uncertainty in his production and marketing operations without also facing the uncertainty of the price of his raw materials. He is thus happy to pay something to remove this uncertainty. Thus, in theory at least, the provision of a lively and efficient futures market by the speculators should be paid for by ensuring a worthwhile return, on average, for the speculators as they are providing a useful service. To the commodity producers and users, the use of the futures market can be thought of as an insurance arrangement. However, there is a difference between an insurance market and a commodity market, as an insurance contract is based upon the prediction of an aggregate—one can predict fairly well the total cost of house fires in a year, for example, but one cannot predict which houses will burn. In a commodity market prices can move only in one direction at a time. So, unlike an insurance company, a speculator on a commodity market has to back his judgement about future price changes. If he is skilled he can do this profitably, particularly if he makes proper use of all of the types of contract and policy available to him in a sensible manner, as described in Chapter 6.

A rather different use of the futures market is known as hedging, which will be dealt with in Chapters 3 and 8. As a very simple example, consider a grain operator in Chicago who buys 10,000 bushels of wheat from farmers on 1 August, at the spot price, minus a discount for storage charges and for acting as a middleman between the farmers and the eventual users of the wheat. He uses the current spot price on the market as a guide, but can pay slightly under this spot price, as if all the farmers attempted to unload their wheat on the market at the same time this would inevitably lower the spot price and thus the sum of money that the farmers could receive. Suppose also that the grain operator finds that present conditions prevent a forward sale of his purchase. He is therefore at risk if spot prices decline and can counteract this by selling on the futures market. If later a spot or forward buyer is found, the futures sell can be matched with a futures buy. The operator's balance sheet may look as follows:

Cash market	*Futures hedge*
Initiating the hedge	
1 Aug: Buys 10,000 bu at $1·75*	1 Aug: Sells 10,000 bu futures at $2·00
Cancelling the hedge	
30 Nov: Sells 10,000 bu at $1·65	30 Nov: Buys 10,000 bu May futures at $1·90
Net gain or loss	
Loss: $0·10/bu	Gain: $0·10/bu

The above is an example of a "short hedge". The asterisk on the $1·75 for the first buy is a reminder that this is the spot price operating on 1 August, but the operator will pay slightly less than this to cover storage costs, etc. This premium, in our example, will represent his profit, after brokers' commissions have been paid. By using the futures market to hedge, he has limited his loss, and in fact managed to maintain his margin. However, in the example, it has been assumed that the cash and futures prices move together perfectly. In reality this is not quite so, and in practice the operator may make a loss or profit on the hedge, but his level of risk will nevertheless have been much reduced.

There are many types of hedge available to producers, holders, exporters and users of commodities, but space does not allow a description of all of the possibilities. It is seen that such hedges are possible only with an active futures market as provided by speculators—in fact the main reason for the existence of a futures market is to allow hedging to occur.

Various academic studies have investigated the effectiveness of hedging. In general, the studies have found hedging to be an effective means of limiting losses against spot price changes, except for small price changes. Thus, hedging proves most effective for the type of price changes that the businessman is most concerned with, those of large magnitude.

HOW THE EXCHANGES OPERATE

The exchange, or terminal market, for a commodity provides a number of services that are vital for the existence of a futures market, such as providing a location for trading and price-making, determining various technical questions such as allowable terminal dates, contract sizes and acceptable grades of the commodity, and also undertaking the settlement procedure.

The method of trading is basically similar for all exchanges, although there are differences in detail. Usually the trading is in circular "rings", either with one such circle for each commodity or with trading at prescribed times if several commodities are traded in the same place. In the majority of cases the dealers face each other and bids and offers are by open outcry, with the double auction principle of rising bids meeting declining offers. Each contract that is reached is publicly recorded and reported in the financial pages of the major newspapers. The auction is carried out between dealers representing the clients of brokers or of major producers and users. In all markets, trading starts with a loud bell, and often at the opening, the close and at certain fixed times during the day dealing is done as "call-overs" through a call chairman. These chairmen keep the markets orderly, declare who has dealt with whom, and maintain proper queue order when more than one firm is bidding or offering at the same price, the principle being "first come, first served". The call-over prices often become the official prices of the market, are widely distributed by the news services and are then used for physical trading around the world. Many of the communist countries, for example, use the prices on the London markets to determine the prices at which they themselves trade.

Many exchanges also have rules about the extent to which a price can change in a given period, in an attempt to limit the extent of price variation in a short time interval. In the cocoa market, for example, if a particularly large price change occurs, the market will close for thirty minutes in the hope that stabilising influences will appear, and in sugar there is a limit of a £5 price change in any 24-hour period.

The settlement house of the exchange notes all of the futures contracts that have been negotiated in the past for a given terminal date, and when this date is reached matches all of the cancelling contracts and determines who has to deliver how much of the commodity to whom. No physical delivery is required, of course, but rather an exchange of title to a quantity of the commodity stored in some storehouse acceptable to the exchange.

More details about the operating procedures of the principal London exchanges will be found in Chapters 4 and 5 and in Appendix 2.

WHAT IS SOLD AND WHERE

A full list of all of the commodities for which futures markets exist is a long and impressive one with over forty items ranging from the prosaic (such as cotton, oats and zinc) to the exotic (silver, coconut oil, shellac) and including the unlikely (propane, mercury, plywood and frozen pork bellies). The large majority of the list are traded in the United States, mostly in New York, Chicago, Minneapolis and Kansas City, but very important exchanges are also found in Sydney (for wool), Paris and the Continent of Europe, and, naturally, London. Although the list of commodities traded is a long one, only a few are sufficiently actively traded for the private investor to be interested in them. In London, the most active markets are in cocoa, coffee and sugar, together with five metals: copper, tin, lead, zinc and silver. Other fairly active London markets are in rubber, wool, wheat, barley and platinum, and special markets are held for much less active commodities such as copra, jute and diamonds. The London exchanges are all situated in a small half-mile square centred on Fenchurch Street in the EC3 district.

The reasons that are generally accepted to be necessary for the existence of a viable futures market include: many suppliers and users of the commodity; co-operation by the trade, who must also use it for hedging; the commodity must be storable, so that a relatively stable relationship between cash and futures prices can exist; and the commodity must be easy to grade and be of an easily determined quality. If production is largely from a single source, such as was true for nickel, a futures market cannot develop, and, if part of the trade is against a futures market, again it cannot exist, petroleum being an example. Despite one being able to list the reasons for the existence of a market, it often happens that a particular commodity market is started but then flops or just manages to hang on without stimulating sufficient interest to make it a really worthwhile market. The reasons for such failures are not always very clear. For example, the Chicago Mercantile Exchange created markets in both ham and bacon: the first was a failure but the second an enormous success.

There always seem to be plans afoot for the creation of further markets, particularly on the West Coast of the United States, where coconut oil has already been successfully launched, and consideration is being given to tomato paste, wine, almonds and tuna fish, for example. In London thoughts are being turned to aluminium and nickel and there is mention of whisky futures, as well as tea.

There is also the possibility of futures markets in non-commodities. A Chicago exchange has already decided to make use of its expertise in futures trading by opening a market in share option futures which could greatly alter the pattern of trading on the New York Stock Exchange and elsewhere. Thought is also being given to ocean-freight-rate futures and mortgage-rate futures although acceptance of these by the general speculator may be rather slow.

Many commodities are traded in several exchanges; for example silver is active in New York, Chicago and London. Naturally, the various markets keep closely in touch with each other. If ever their prices should drift sufficiently far apart, traders will arbitrage between them, buying on one and immediately selling on the other, until the prices are brought together again, provided problems such as currency exchange restrictions can be profitably overcome.

Chapter 3

Types of Trading

P. J. CORNISH

Managing Director, Commodity Management Services Ltd

The investor is interested in commodities not because he wants to sell or process wool or zinc but because commodity futures, with their wide price movements over relatively short time-periods, offer an unrivalled investment medium for "risk capital".

Commodities are traded either on the physical markets for current use (when the seller has current possession and the buyer requires delivery immediately) or on the futures markets—alternatively called "terminal markets" in the United Kingdom—where contracts are traded for the delivery of a commodity at some stated month in the future.* It is the latter market that is of particular interest to the investor.

HOW THE FUTURES MARKETS ARE USED

There are two principal uses of the futures markets, hedging and speculation, as well as a third, buying and selling.

Hedging

As discussed in Chapter 2, the reason for the existence of the futures markets is the inexpensive and secure protection they can offer against price variations to farmers, producers, processors, exporters/importers and manufacturers. This protection is termed a hedge: it lays off the risk that the price of a commodity will, at some future time, rise or fall from current levels. A simple definition of a hedge is "the opening of a futures position opposite to that held in the physical commodity".

A hedger can be a producer, processor or consumer of commodities—anyone who deals in them. He views the commodity markets strictly as a

---

* "Physicals" are also traded on the futures markets, at all times on the London Metal Exchange and are tenderable for soft commodities when the current month is a delivery month.

vehicle by which he can establish and safeguard his future price commitments, not as a place to make a profit. Hedging is insurance to him and he uses the futures market to "balance his books": he offsets a vulnerable position in the physical market by means of an opposite position—a temporary one—in the futures market. The hedger is interested in safeguarding against one of two fundamental risks.

1. *The risk that the value of unsold products will depreciate if commodity prices fall*
This risk is offset by a forward sale on the futures markets: a "short hedge". For instance, if the commodity price starts to decline, a processor or manufacturer would begin to lose money in respect of the physical stock he owns of that commodity. He gains, however, commensurately, from his short hedge, in that, the lower the price moves, the less he will eventually have to pay to liquidate it, or close out his position. This latter gain—if his hedge equals his physical stock in size—should exactly counterbalance the loss he is incurring on his physical stock. Similarly, should the price rise after he placed his short hedge, the increase in value of his stock, which can then be sold at correspondingly high prices, offsets the loss incurred by the short hedge. A short hedge is used by farmers, producers, manufacturers and merchants.

EXAMPLE
On 26 July a firm of wiredrawers (who process metal bars into rods and coils of wire) buys 50 tons of copper wirebars at a price of £833 per ton (total cost £41,650). By the nature of the finished product, the price at which the firm will be able to sell it will depend heavily on the price of copper at that time and is—essentially—the price of copper bars plus the cost of extrusion into wire plus the firm's normal operating profit.

Therefore, from the time the wiredrawers purchase their 50 tons of bars to the time, about a month later, they sell the coils, they are vulnerable to a fall in the price of copper. To ensure against loss in such an eventuality, the firm hedges. It sells short, at the time of purchase, two lots (50 tons) of three-month copper futures at £816 per ton (total £40,800).

On 24 August it contracts to sell, in rod form, the 50 tons of bars, at a price based on the last official LME spot price of copper, £786 per ton. Its incremental costs are £20 per ton. The price is £806 per ton (total £40,300). Ostensibly the firm will thereupon incur a loss on this transaction of £1350. In fact, however, the hedge was closed on 24 August, by buying back the two lots of copper at £780 per ton (£39,000). The hedge generated a profit of £1800 (excluding commission).

2. *The risk that forward sales will show losses if commodity prices rise*
This risk can be covered by a forward purchase on the futures markets: a "long hedge". A long hedge is of interest to someone like an exporter, who contracts forward to supply his commodity at the current price;

because shipment is not until some future time, he does not know what will then be the market price. It is possible for him to buy the commodity immediately he signs the contract and store it, but this step involves tying up capital and incurring storage and insurance charges. Alternatively, he could wait until shipment, in which case—should prices have risen in the interval—he would suffer financial loss. Either possibility is avoided by purchasing the required tonnage on the futures market. If the price falls by the time he makes shipment, he will show a loss on the futures trans-action but will be able to purchase the spot commodity cheaper. Should the market rise, he will have an equivalent profit on his futures position to compensate for the higher price of the physical commodity.

A long hedge would also be employed by a manufacturer who fixes his selling prices and current contracts for future delivery based on current costs and whose profits therefore would suffer should his raw materials subsequently increase in cost.

EXAMPLE

A miller has received an order from a baker in July for milled flour, delivery to be in October (the price of the flour would be based on the then-current price of wheat plus the cost of processing as well as the miller's normal profit). Because the miller does not yet own the wheat to be milled, 100 tons in all, as soon as he signs the contract committing himself to deliver (at a fixed price) a commodity he does not yet own, he is at risk. Should the price of the com-modity then rise, his costs will too, and his profit diminish.

Of course, if the price falls, his profit will increase to the same degree. However, the miller does not wish to bear such a risk and goes to the futures markets to lay it off.

On the same day he signs the contract, 13 July, he buys one lot of "September wheat", of 100 tons, at £48·90 per ton. He has thereby hedged his risk until September, when he will purchase the 100 tons of wheat necessary to fulfil the order by October. He must make his purchase on 14 September, the date having been determined by his mill's capacity and backlog.

By this date, however, wheat prices have risen, from the £48·90 per ton obtained on 13 July, to £59·65 per ton for the soft milling wheat he will require. For the 100 tons the miller needs, he must pay an extra £1075—*i.e.* 100 × £(59·65 − 48·90). Had the miller not hedged, he might have obliterated his operating profit, but in this case he has his "September wheat" contract, which he sells on 14 September for £58·90 per ton, providing him with a hedging profit of £1000, virtually matching the £1075 loss he has incurred by the rise in wheat prices. Had the price dropped between 13 July and 14 Septem-ber, the miller would have made a loss on his September futures position, but—as the price of his milling wheat would have also dropped—that loss would have been balanced by the lower cost of his raw material.

It is noteworthy that with neither instance of hedging is there a need to take delivery of the commodity from, or to deliver it to, the futures market.

In addition to avoiding these two risks, hedging offers a further advantage
to the businessman. In the normal course of business, it is often useful to
obtain advances against inventories. Such inventories as a matter of course
are covered by insurance against the risk of fire, water damage or spoilage,
but, when they are also covered by hedging against the risk of an adverse
price fluctuation, banks tend to take a favourable attitude, and, by obtaining larger working capital from banks, turnover can be more rapid and
profits increased.

Speculation

Hedging, as we have seen, deliberately eliminates the possibility of a gain
in order to safeguard against a loss. In contrast, the second principal user
of the futures markets, the speculator, enters the commodity field specifically to risk his capital in the expectation that he will create dealing profits.
By supplying his capital, he helps create the liquidity necessary for the
hedgers to be able to offset their risks.

"Speculation" has assumed a pejorative meaning: obtaining excessive
profits. In so far as commodity futures are concerned, the derogatory
definition does not apply: profits are earned, by placing capital at risk.
The speculator enters the market specifically to assume the risk that the
hedger does not wish to bear.

Buying and selling

There is a final category of person—other than the hedger or speculator—
who utilises the futures markets: the buyer or seller. In this sense, the
markets perform the same service as the physical or "spot" market, except
that buyer and seller do not meet and that the commodity is tenderable
at up to eighteen months distance in time. Because there is a time lapse
between the bargain being struck and delivery, either party is free to change
his mind and reverse it, unlike on the physical markets. (There are disadvantages, however, to this use of the futures markets, which will be
discussed further.) In this regard, the futures markets, aside from providing
a forum for buyers and sellers to meet, have created an accurate and respon-
sive price-information service, publicising commodity prices for any
particular period from the present up to a year and a half in the future.

FUTURES TRADING

At first sight the futures markets operate on much the same principle as
the Stock Exchange:

1. They bring buyers and sellers together.
2. They provide a forum where prices are fixed and can be ascertained.

3. They allow quick, public and uncomplicated trading, according to agreed rules and practices and at fixed brokerage charges.
4. They stipulate a "quality control" in that—like the Stock Exchange, where a company must meet certain standards for its shares to be traded—the quality and quantity of the commodity tendered must meet or exceed specified standards set by a quality control committee.

The essential difference between the two types of market, however, is that securities denoting ownership of equity are traded on the Stock Exchange, whereas on the futures markets are traded contracts ("a commitment to deliver or receive a specific type and amount of commodity at a specific time to one of several specific places"). The contract does not signify ownership, but an explicit promise that on the delivery date the registered holder of a short contract will tender the commodity in accordance with the rules of the applicable clearing house and that the registered holder of a long contract on the spot date will receive tender.

Because ownership of the commodity is not yet represented by the futures contract (that is, not unless the investor—shortly before the spot date—decides he wishes to deliver or take possession), there is no need to consider such problems as deterioration, loss, fire or water damage, quality, storage or shipment of the commodity. Similarly there is no benefit of dividends, warrants or rights.

A variety of commodities are traded on the London futures markets. They are generally classified according to the following groups:

"Soft commodities"	*Metals*
Cocoa	Base:
Sugar	Copper (wirebars and cathodes)
Coffee (Robusta and Arabica)	Lead
Grains (wheat and barley)	Zinc
Wool	Tin
Soyabean oil	Noble:
Palm oil	Silver
Rubber*	

* In this book, because of certain features peculiar to the rubber trade, for convenience rubber will be considered in Chapter 5 with metals and bullion, and not with the other soft commodities in Chapter 4—*Editor.*

Of these, cocoa, sugar and copper are the most heavily traded, with lead, zinc, silver, coffee and rubber coming next. Appendix 2 sets out the basic trading information for each commodity.

An integral part of all futures markets, with the exception of the London Metal Exchange, is the clearing house, which is usually a private incorporated association, whose purposes are, *inter alia*: to check, settle and report the day's business on the exchange; to guarantee fulfilment, against default, of each contract made on the exchange; to assign tenders and re-tenders.

The International Commodities Clearing House Ltd (ICCH) fulfils these functions for all the soft commodities (with the exception of rubber —but see Chapter 5) traded on the London futures markets. All members of the ICCH are also members of the various exchanges and any business on the exchanges must be conducted through an ICCH member.

Business on the various exchanges is conducted with the appropriate clearing house always acting as intermediary. That is, when two brokers have traded on the floor of the exchange, the contracts are "cleared" by the clearing house and, provided that the brokers confirm their acceptance of this business, then these contracts are registered in the names of these brokers by the clearing house, which then guarantees their due fulfilment. This system eliminates worry about the future solvency of a broker with whom one has traded, because the other party to the trade is always the clearing house.

Each member of the clearing house puts up an original margin or deposit upon election to membership and—in the event of wide adverse price fluctuations—may be called upon to furnish an additional margin. Settlement of contracts is done not broker-to-broker but always with the clearing house. It is done on a daily basis, in cash.

PHYSICAL TRADING

As noted above, the futures markets are used, not only to hedge and fix future prices, but to buy and sell commodities for actual use at some future time. In practice, however, the futures markets are rarely utilised for this last purpose.* The physical markets provide more flexibility: the size of contract traded is not fixed, as on the futures markets, and a deal of virtually any size may be consummated on the physical markets. Another point is that a futures contract does not specify the exact type of commodity traded (*e.g.* Ghana as against Ivory Coast cocoa beans) and therefore the precise requirements of the purchaser may not be met in this regard. Finally, the location of a commodity tendered on the futures market may not be where the purchaser wants (*e.g.* coffee tendered on the London Coffee Terminal Market can be from warehouses in Amsterdam, Rotterdam or Hamburg). These three factors—concerning contract size,

* The London Metal Exchange is an exception. The LME trades metals for all dates from "cash metal" (*i.e.* due for delivery in an LME-registered warehouse on the following business day) to "three months".

type and location of commodities—render the futures markets less attractive than the physical markets for dealing in "actuals".

Despite these factors, none the less, there can be times when it would pay the investor to take delivery of a commodity on the futures market and store it for resale on the futures or physical market later. One such time would be when the contango between near and distant delivery months is greater than the costs of taking delivery of the near month and storing the commodity until the distant month. Another might be when the investor, holding a long position about to become spot, is faced with what he believes to be a temporary low price for his commodity. Rather than close out at this low level, he would prefer to take delivery and re-tender later when the price has recovered.

When considering such a possible course of action, the investor should consider the following additional costs involved in taking delivery:

1. *The cost of money.* When taking delivery, the investor must pay the total amount of the contract—roughly ten times his original margin. Irrespective of whether the investor borrows money for the duration of the time he stores the commodity (and pays interest on the borrowing) or whether he utilises his own capital (and loses the interest he might otherwise be earning on that amount), he must include this cost in his calculations.
2. *The cost of storage.* Once he takes possession of the commodity, the investor is responsible for paying the rental of warehouse space, as well as for paying fire insurance. Both costs tend to fluctuate with inflation and, in the case of continental warehouses, currency-rate changes, but up-to-date quotations are easily and quickly obtained through any broker. These costs are payable to the clearing house and are charged on a daily basis.*
3. *Freight.* A possible additional cost factor arises from price differentials at different locations. (For example, cocoa located in Liverpool is more valuable to Rowntrees than Amsterdam cocoa, and the converse applies to Nestlés.) The investor should be aware of the marginal gain or loss involved in accepting tender from a far-distant warehouse.

Grading
A point of critical concern to anyone taking delivery of a commodity is assurance of quality.

In order for a soft commodity to be accepted by the clearing house for

---

* Depending on the date tender is accepted during the spot month, from one to twenty-eight days of the fire insurance premium may already have been paid by the tenderer. This "free coverage" is passed on, in the event of re-tender.

tender, it must be graded, and, as stated above, one of the functions of the clearing house is to assess each and every lot tendered to ensure it meets the standards set for the commodity. If the standards are not met, then the commodity is untenderable.

Trading on the LME, either of physicals or futures, is restricted to metals approved by and registered with the exchange (actually by the Committee of Subscribers, an elected body of LME members, who are charged with the administration of the LME). Such approval is given only after analysis by two different assayers, registered with the LME, after an undertaking is given by the tenderer that the sample analysed fairly represents the metal to be tendered, and after testimony is received from two consumers that the metal in question is suitable for use.

The metals must be in a specified form and of a certain quality (*e.g.* copper wirebars must be either electrolytic copper or High Conductivity Fire Refined Copper, of standard dimensions in the weight range of 90–125 kg). Metals achieving these standards are branded (stamped) and can be traded and re-traded on the LME.

For soft commodities, each market association has appointed Grading Committees, each comprising about twenty members. Depending on the volume of grading to be done, these are split into smaller committees all operating at the same time. The minimum number required to judge a lot is two members, and no person who is termed an "interested party" in the commodity to be graded may act as a grader. There is no appeal against the Committee's decision, although there is a procedure for a later review, at a nominal fee, in the event of the commodity having been declared untenderable.

Out of each lot offered for tender the graders take a sample and test it for, *inter alia*, colour, smell, appearance, extraneous matter and spoilage. If it passes, the lot is awarded a Certificate of Quality. This certificate is valid for six months (unless the commodity is moved from its warehouse during that time) and is proof that the lot is tenderable and re-tenderable to the ICCH. It is important to note, however, that the certificate is not evidence of the exact type of commodity, merely that the commodity is tenderable and is of a certain quality. If the lot is judged to exceed the minimum standards of the association, the Grading Committee places on it an allowance over the contract price (*e.g.* £2 per ton), to be paid by the deliveree. This premium, however, is passed on at the re-tender. A deduction is likewise made in the event of the lot being marginally inferior.

There is a further risk that an investor must consider in respect of taking delivery: the risk that, after he has held the commodity for six months, it will not receive a renewed Certificate of Quality, owing to deterioration.

Unlike the case of other soft commodities, no investor may take delivery of sugar in the United Kingdom. The London Sugar Market permits only dealers to do so—specifically only the firms of Tate & Lyle, the British Sugar Corporation and Manbré & Garton. Should an investor decide that it would be advantageous to hold physical sugar, he would do so through the clearing house in the Paris or New York markets and storage would be in the warehouses licensed with the appropriate markets (*e.g.* Dunkirk for Paris). Bank of England approval is required for the British investor to take such a step and—because of the investment currency requirements in addition to the costs of storage and insurance—it is improbable that taking delivery of sugar would be of interest to the investor.

The example of cocoa

The procedure for taking delivery of soft commodities other than sugar differs only in detail; the example of cocoa is applicable generally.

If an investor decides not to close a futures contract as his delivery month approaches but to hold it for delivery (for a long contract), he gives notice, through his broker, to the ICCH, in this example, that he will accept tender. At any time during the delivery month, therefore, his broker will accept on his behalf (but in its own name).

The investor must accept the first tender offered or his long position will be liquidated; he cannot wait and choose between tenders. Upon acceptance, the investor has up to fourteen days to make full payment for his purchase. When he pays the ICCH for his cocoa, he receives a Warehouse Warrant, which in effect is a depository receipt, a document of ownership of a specific lot of cocoa in a designated warehouse. (It is also a demand note in that, when produced to the warehouseman, it permits the investor—should he wish—to move the cocoa.)

The Warrant and the Certificate of Quality are all that is required to re-tender the cocoa on the spot market.

OPTIONS

At the other end of the trading spectrum from taking delivery of a commodity is option trading. Options are traded on both the Stock Exchange and the commodity futures markets and on each they offer the same attraction: they provide the only certain means of limiting risk.

Commodity options have been traded in London since before the Second World War and constitute a small but significant portion (approximately 5 per cent) of the business of the London commodity exchanges. The advantages of limiting risk apply to both sides of an option contract and can be briefly explained as follows:

1. *From the granter's side*. It is likely that the granter of an option would be a big dealer or more likely a manufacturer with large physical stocks. The advantage of writing an option is not only that his stocks

are hedged on the futures market but also that he stands to gain the premium income when the option is declared, whether he has to deliver a futures contract or eventually physical goods against it, or if the contract is abandoned. This premium income is useful to the manufacturer as it can enable him to lower his prices because the premium income should in effect have reduced his raw material costs.

2. *From the taker's point of view.* An option contract is an attraction particularly in markets where it is difficult to see any definite market trends. For the privilege the taker must pay a premium, but the amount of premium means that this is the maximum amount that the taker can lose on his contract. If the option trade turns out to show him a loss he will abandon it, and so it can be said that the premium money is a form of insurance payment.

It should also be emphasised that many traders who both grant and take options will trade against them by buying and selling normal contracts on the futures market. This is obviously a sophisticated operation and not one an investor should carry out without a good knowledge of what is involved and the advice of a competent broker.

For certain commodities—namely cocoa, coffee, sugar and wool—the ICCH guarantees option contracts in exactly the same way that they guarantee normal contracts. The taker pays the premium money to the ICCH, where it is held in a special interest-earning account for the granter and is not released during the life of an option. The above does not apply for the London Metal Exchange or the London Rubber Market, who do not use the services of the ICCH. (As mentioned elsewhere in this book, the rubber trade will from late 1974 employ the services of the ICCH for clearing and guaranteeing all their contracts which would include options.)

In principle, trading in commodity options is the same as trading in share options. However, the few differences should be noted.

First, the life of a commodity option, which can be from thirty days (for, say, silver) to three years (for rubber), is more flexible and generally of longer duration than share options, which are usually for three months.

Second, the price of a commodity option is usually lower with all costs considered (share transactions are subject to stamp duty; those in commodities are not). A share option might run 8 to 20 per cent of the share price. Over the year, this represents from 32 to 80 per cent of the share price. In contrast, a commodity "put" or "call" option costs around 5 to 15 per cent of the price of the commodity and can be negotiated for a delivery month up to eighteen months or more away.

The salient attraction of options, however, arises from the fact that, although the investor's risk or liability is limited to the amount of his premium, the potential profits to be gained can be substantial.

Purchasing options means that the investor is buying time. For this privilege a premium over an agreed "basis" or "striking" price is paid. It follows that the cost of this premium depends upon how far forward the investor wishes to deal and it varies from market to market.

Options are traded in three forms: "calls", "puts" and "doubles".

1. *A "call" option* gives the buyer the right to buy at the basis price at any time between the date of purchasing the option and the expiry date. This option would suit an investor who expects the market to rise but wants to limit his loss should things go wrong.
2. *A "put" option* is the reverse, giving the buyer the right to sell at the basis price at any time between the date of purchasing and the expiry date. It is taken out when a decline is expected.
3. *A "double" option* works both ways, when the investor expects to make money whichever way the market moves—although, as the name implies, the premium is usually twice the amount of that for the other options.

For example, suppose an investor expects to see a fall in the cocoa market by the end of the year. He negotiates through his broker to buy a put. Assume that the current market value for December cocoa is £580 per ton. The buyer agrees to pay a premium of £55 a ton over the current market value to secure the call. For five lots, 50 tons, the purchaser pays £2750 plus commission. If, between the day of striking and the expiration of the option, December cocoa trades below £522·50 per ton, a profit is made by declaring the option, inclusive of £2·50 per ton total commission. Whereupon the granter of the option must send him a contract for December cocoa sold at £580 per ton.

For a call option to be profitable, the market would have to rise by a similar amount, and the seller of the call would then send a contract for December cocoa at £580 per ton.

A further advantage of trading in options is the ability to convert without incurring risk. In the above example, suppose that, after the investor has purchased five lots of puts, the market falls to £500 per ton. The investor will be showing a good profit and if he thinks that a reaction is imminent he can buy, say, three lots to protect himself. This secures an automatic profit. If the market continues to fall, his profit is limited to two puts. But should the market rebound from the £500 per ton level where he bought three lots, he can wait until the market looks ready to resume its major trend and sell his three "longs". He has therefore reinstated his original five put options and taken a profit out of the market by trading against his option position without incurring any further outlay of capital or increasing his risk.

In uncertain market conditions double options are particularly useful as the purchaser has the right to put or call the commodity on to the seller. In the example above he may pay a £110 per ton premium for the double option at a basis price of £580 for December. The market must then move either below £470 or above £690 per ton for him to make a profit.

By the correct use of options the investor can take a more speculative view of the markets, knowing that he has a limit on his losses. Once a market is in an established trend it generally takes a major event to reverse this movement. But by studying the daily commodity reports the investor can anticipate minor trend changes by trading against his option, and in so doing it is common for worthwhile profits to be made well before the option is due to expire.

Over recent years there have been very few occasions when the markets have not moved enough to cover the double option premium: most have given an excellent return.

There are times when, owing to expectations of future market performance, granters of options become unwilling to sell puts or calls, or place an unattractively high premium on the one over the other. In such a case the investor can create his own double option. Thus, two calls can be converted into one double by selling a futures contract on the market at the time the calls are purchased. If the market moves up, one of the original calls "hedges" the short sale, while the other call is making a profit. If the market drops, neither call becomes operative, while the "short" makes a profit. A similar result applies to buying two puts and a "long" against one of them.

Yet another way of profiting from option trading is to sell an option, having previously purchased one. For example, an investor may buy a March coffee call, basis price £480 per ton, at a premium of, say, £33. If the market moves to only £500 and looks as if it will advance no further, there is no profit. However, it could be possible to sell a March call option on the market, at the current basis price of £500, for the same premium. There is no risk: the investor retains his first option, and, if the market goes up and the second is called, he takes as profit the difference between the two basis prices, £20 per ton. If the market sits, he has at least recovered his costs.

Chapter 4

Soft Commodities

M. E. T. DAVIES
Managing Director, Inter Commodities Ltd

The term "soft commodites" encompasses nearly every commodity of size, other than metals, traded in an organised market. The soft commodity markets of more interest to the outside investor are those with large and active futures markets. The only markets trading actively in London today that fall into this category are those for cocoa, sugar, coffee, wheat, barley, vegetable oils and wool. There are large markets in other soft commodities such as tea, cotton, jute, hides and furs, etc., but these markets deal in the physical commodity and have no organised futures markets. This chapter, therefore, proposes to deal to a greater extent with the commodities in which there is organised and regulated forward dealing.

DEVELOPMENT OF MARKETS

Before dealing with each of the futures markets in detail, it would be as well to explain how the organised markets developed. Commodity exchanges came into being during the nineteenth century, following the rapid expansion of national economies. Improved methods of communication, scientific discoveries and the rapid growth in population caused a huge increase in international trade. Business began to have a more international flavour and the raw materials for industry were no longer affected only by local conditions. There was greater competition between primary producers for markets and, more important, an extension in the time-period between initial production and final sale.

To ensure an even flow of finished produce, merchants, dealers and manufacturers were forced to hold a much larger stock of raw materials, which exposed them to greater financial risk, and, as companies operated mainly on borrowed capital, any adverse price movement could have a disastrous effect on their liquidity. Thus, it was necessary to find a means of limiting the risks to which producers and users of raw materials were

31

constantly exposed. The result was that primitive exchanges grew up in City coffee shops where merchants, shippers and processors met to do business. Trading first came under one roof in 1811, when the Commercial Sale Rooms were opened.

Futures trading had its beginnings in the "soft commodity" of cotton, which was largely traded in Liverpool. The large majority of the cotton exported to the United Kingdom was imported from the Americas by merchants to Liverpool. These merchants were stockholders who kept large supplies not far from the spinners' mills. A large proportion of the spinners ran small businesses: therefore they were not able to carry large stocks and were very dependent on the credit given by the dealers. During the American Civil War supplies began to dry up, and, to meet the enlarged demand from speculators and traders, cotton contracts began to be concluded for much later periods than had previously been the case. People started dealing in cotton "yet to be shipped" and it is this phrase that shows the beginnings of the futures markets. A sophisticated cotton futures market was developed, but subsequently, as has been the case with several commodities, government intervention in the physical market killed the futures market to the detriment of the whole industry, and at the moment there is no active cotton futures market in the United Kingdom. There was an attempt to reinstate one a few years ago, but this proved abortive. However, in the United States, there are active cotton futures markets in New York and Chicago.

COCOA

Background
One of the most active and talked-about commodity futures markets in the United Kingdom is the London Cocoa Terminal Market. The cocoa plant seems to have originated in the Americas and, most probably, in the Amazon basin. The first Spaniards to land in Mexico discovered that it had been in use there for many years and in fact it played an important role in the Aztec and other Indian tribes' religion. It was believed that Quetzalcoatl, a figure in Mayan Indian legend, brought the original seeds from Paradise. Long before Columbus discovered America, cocoa beans (or seeds) were used to prepare a frothy drink which the early inhabitants of Mexico called *chocolatl* (a compound of the Mayan words "*choco*", "warm", and *latl*, "beverage"). Although cocoa was considered by some to be an aphrodisiac, its bitter taste made it unpopular with the Spanish traders and settlers. It was only with the introduction of sugar that it became popular in Spain, and Maria Theresa is said to have started a fashion with it at the French Court after her marriage to Louis XIV.

Gradually the drinking of cocoa spread throughout Europe, although it did not gain real popularity until the middle of the nineteenth century when a method of preparing cocoa powder by removing most of the cocoa butter was discovered, thus making it a much lighter drink. It was about this time that it ceased to become only a drink and was turned into edible chocolate bars.

In cocoa's early days, it was mainly grown in the tropical areas of the South American continent with Venezuela being perhaps the largest producer and exporter. By the middle of the eighteenth century, cocoa had been planted in Bahia (Brazil) and a little later was being taken by Spanish sailors to the Philippines and to Fernando Po and other islands off the coast of Africa. It is said that in the middle of the nineteenth century a blacksmith visiting Fernando Po from the Gold Coast (now Ghana) was impressed by the rewards of growing cocoa and took a pod home with him. Out of this one pod grew the backbone of the Gold Coast's economy and the main supply of cocoa to the world. In 1900 the West Indies and the Americas produced nearly 75 per cent of the world's net cocoa-bean exports, but from 1900 onwards cocoa production increased greatly in the Gold Coast and other West African regions. By the early 1920s Africa's net cocoa-bean exports exceeded the combined shipments of the rest of the world, and by the mid 1960s Africa accounted for nearly 75 per cent of all raw-cocoa shipments.

Brazil is now the largest non-African exporter of cocoa, and the bulk of her cocoa, which has a different taste to that of African cocoa, goes to the United States. It is virtually all grown in the Bahia area of Brazil on large estates with the marketing being handled by the Bahia State Marketing Board. The main crop is harvested between September and January and a smaller mid-crop between mid April and August. In Africa, the next-largest producers to Ghana are Nigeria and the Ivory Coast, and the main crop of all three of these countries is harvested between September and February and the mid-crop from April to June.

In Ghana cocoa is largely grown on smallholdings by small-scale farmers and the marketing done by the Ghana Cocoa State Marketing Board. During the main crop, they issue a weekly figure stating how much cocoa they have bought from the farmers. This weekly purchase figure gives a good idea of how production is progressing and is always eagerly awaited by the followers of the cocoa market.

Cocoa requires a warm, humid atmosphere, a well-distributed rainfall (between 50 and 200 inches per annum, depending on the soil drainage conditions) and an annual average temperature of about $25°$ Centigrade. It is important that the farmers exercise good husbandry by spraying their crops, as cocoa is subject to many fast-spreading diseases, the worst of which are the swollen-shoot virus, the toxic capsid bug and certain toxic fungus infections such as black pod and witches' broom.

The market

Futures trading in cocoa began as the result of the sharp increase in trade in the physical commodity during the boom which followed the First World War. As production grew so did dealers' warehouse stocks, and so the need to hedge stocks and commitments was felt by everyone concerned with the industry. The Cocoa Association of London was formed in 1926, a year after the formation of a futures market in New York. However, it was not until two years later that the London Cocoa Terminal Market Association was opened. The market was mainly used by the trade and there was not the outside speculation that there is today. The volume was somewhat erratic during the years up to the Second World War, but 1937 saw the best volume when 352,250 tons were traded. From 1940 to 1950 the price of cocoa was controlled by the Ministry of Food, as was its

Table 4.1. Cocoa: London futures transactions,
1951–73

Year	Transactions (in long tons)	Transactions (in tonnes)
1951	52,265	
1952	121,850	
1953	146,420	
1954	284,795	
1955	191,225	
1956	211,920	
1957	222,290	
1958	365,110	
1959	292,850	
1960	257,890	
1961	420,410	
1962	459,395	
1963	901,550	
1964	712,210	
1965	1,243,680	
1966	1,946,155	
1967	2,085,000	
1968	3,540,000	
1969	4,970,000	
1970	5,646,260	
1971	5,144,740	
1972	5,026,830	225,690
1973	1,951,390	9,647,280

Source: International Commodities Clearing House Ltd

distribution. Futures trading started again in 1951 and the volume of business steadily grew, but gathered greater momentum in the late 1960s when shortages in the physical commodity resulted in an increased use of the futures market, as can be seen from Table 4.1.

The contract is for 10 tonnes (or 1000 kg or 2204·60 lb avoirdupois) or for multiples of 10 tonnes of cocoa beans of a growth and quality as defined in detail in the Rules of the Association, delivered at contract price ex-warehouse approved by the Association in London, Liverpool, Avonmouth, Hull or the Borough of Teesside, or delivered in approved warehouses in Amsterdam, Antwerp, Hamburg or Rotterdam. Dealing is up to fifteen months forward in the following delivery months: March, May, July, September and December. Trading is done by open outcry with buyers and sellers matching bids with offers on the floor of the Cocoa Exchange, which is housed in the Corn Exchange Building in Mark Lane.

The market opens at 10.00 a.m., when business is conducted through a Chairman who reads out the name of each buyer and seller and the bargain struck. This call usually lasts for about fifteen minutes but basically goes on until all business has been done. The Chairman then calls out the last buyer's and seller's prices in each month, which serves as a record of the price at that particular time. Trading continues between brokers, but not through the Chairman, until 12.50 p.m., when there is another call, finishing at 1.00 p.m., at which time the market closes until 2.30 p.m. There is another official call at 3.30 p.m. and a final one at 4.50 p.m. At any time during the day, the Chairman may be called for and business conducted through him should market conditions get hectic.

The Chairman records all business transacted through him on the call on a Daily Sheet, which is accessible to all members of the market. The sellers in each transaction have to record each deal done between calls on slips which are handed to the Chairman, who adds the business to the Daily Sheet. The role of the International Commodities Clearing House is described elsewhere in this book (*see* Chapter 3), and it is from these Daily Sheets that it extracts the business of each broker and home member.

There are four types of membership to the market. The first two groups are broker members and home members who are allowed to trade on the floor with each other free of commission. Home members, unlike broker members, are not allowed to do business for each other. The rules of the market allow a maximum of eighteen broker members and thirty-six home members, and home membership is always in the name of the company, whereas broker membership is in the name of the individual. The second two groups are associate and overseas members. These members are not allowed access to deal on the floor, nor are they allowed to deal among themselves, but have to pass contracts directly through one of the other categories of broker. However, they deal at half the rate of

36   *Trading in commodities*

commission payable by a non-member. A non-member's commission is
£24 per lot traded (£12 buying, £12 selling).

If the price of cocoa is bid over or offered over at more than £20 per tonne
from the previous day's closing buyer's price, trading is halted for a period
of thirty minutes, after which it recommences with a special call; from
then on there is no limit during the rest of the day. It should be noted that
there is never any limit to the extent prices may move on the final call
during the day.

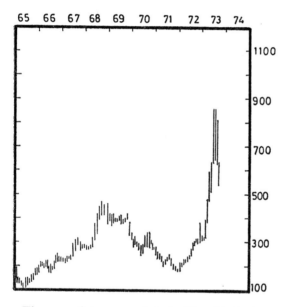

Fig. 4.1. Cocoa:
monthly range of spot
prices, 1965–October
1973 (in £/long ton).

There are futures markets in New York, Amsterdam and Paris, as well
as in London, but the London and New York markets are by far the
largest with roughly the same turnover as each other. There is a large
arbitrage business done between the two markets, but this would not be of
interest to the private speculator unless he had ample funds in both centres
to cover his positions.

Cocoa has always been attractive to the outside speculator, because of
the smallness of the contract size and the wide variation of the price
movements that this seasonal crop has. These large fluctuations in price
have caused some spectacular profits and losses resulting in much publicity.
However, if used sensibly and with the advice of a good broker, the cocoa
market can be a rational form of higher-risk investment. The movements
in future may not be as great as they have been, since in 1973 an International Cocoa Agreement was agreed in Geneva, after many years of

abortive negotiations. However, as the United States has not signed this agreement, there are many who doubt its effectiveness. At the end of 1973 the price of cocoa was way above the proposed ceiling price and, as no buffer stock had yet been built up, it seemed as if it would be some time before the agreement has an effect on prices, if ever.

SUGAR

Background

Unlike cocoa, sugar has been controlled by various agreements for many years, and this is because sugar is a basic and vital foodstuff whereas cocoa is not. It is ironic that in 1973, the year in which a cocoa agreement was hammered out, the International Sugar Agreement should fail to be renegotiated. Commodity agreements are very fine things on paper, but in practice they rarely work or last for long. Of necessity, they must favour the producer, for, in years of plenty, prices may be subsidised and guaranteed, but in years of famine more of the commodity cannot be created and in these years some producers always break the agreement to sell at an agreed price in order to sell at a higher one. In practice, it is much better to let the free market forces take their own course and, if necessary, offer some other form of assistance to developing nations instead of commodity agreements. Only about 15 per cent of total world sales is sold on the free market. The rest is traded under some form of agreement or government-to-government barter deal. Although with the ending of the International Sugar Agreement it will no longer be so much the case, up until 1973 the world price of sugar from year to year was based on what was left at the bottom of the bin after all long-term marketing arrangements.

Sugar is both produced and consumed in virtually every country in the world but found its way to the United Kingdom in quantity in the form of cane sugar from the West Indies in the eighteenth century. The extraction of sugar from beetroot was first discovered by a German chemist named Marggraff in the middle of the eighteenth century, but this was not greatly utilised until the United Kingdom forced it by blockading Napoleon and Europe in the early 1800s. In 1914 three-quarters of the United Kingdom's sugar imports came from Europe and much of it from countries who were to be its enemies in the ensuing war. As a result of this lesson, by the outbreak of the Second World War nearly two-thirds of the United Kingdom's sugar consumption was either domestically or Empire grown. The Commonwealth Sugar Agreement of 1951 gave a large share of the UK market to the Commonwealth at an annually negotiated price which would ensure a "reasonably remunerative price to efficient producers".

The United Kingdom's entry into the EEC has resulted in the phasing

Trading in commodities

out of the Commonwealth Sugar Agreement and more of its sugar will in future come from Europe, which produces enough for its own needs. The exact mechanics of this changeover are the subject of heated political argument, and sugar, which, as in its early days because of its association with the slave trade, once again has found itself the subject of international political disagreement.

The market

The world's first sugar exchange was opened in Hamburg in 1880 as a direct result of the large rise in European beet production. The London market in sugar futures was established in 1888 with a contract unit of 400 tons of raw beet sugar f.o.b.* Hamburg. The market was closed during the First World War and did not reopen until the middle of 1921, when the contract was changed to units of 50 tons white sugar ex bonded warehouse, London. The change in the tariff structure in 1929 meant that virtually no refined sugar was imported, and so a raw sugar contract was brought into being. The market was closed again at the beginning of the Second World War. The Government kept firm control of sugar after the ending of hostilities and were very cautious about returning the trading of what was essentially a dollar commodity into private hands. Controls were not relaxed until 1956 and the United Sugar Terminal Market Association opened at the beginning of 1957 with a contract much the same as that in existence before the war. The present contract, which has been in operation since 1959, is for lots of 50 tons of non-preferential raw cane sugar of 96 degrees polarisation, in bags, delivered c.i.f.† London or Liverpool at the option of the seller and payable in sterling. The seller also has the option to deliver in bulk or deliver preferential-duty sugar at the appropriate adjustments in price.

Delivery may be made against a futures contract on any day of the month in which the contract expires. However, in practice the market is only a paper market as sugar is virtually never delivered to or taken from the market in settlement of a contract. Trading is in contracts for up to one year ahead, of which March, May, August, October and December are the delivery months.

There are thirty full members of the exchange although the rules allow there to be up to sixty-five. Full membership is personal and allows the member or representatives of his firm to deal on the floor of the exchange paying only the International Commodities Clearing House fees. Associate,

---

* f.o.b. stands for "free on board", meaning that the cost of transportation to the point of destination is not included in the quoted price of the commodity.

† c.i.f. indicates that the "cost, insurance and freight" paid at the point of destination is included in the price quoted.

Liverpool affiliated and overseas affiliated members are allowed to deal at a lower rate of commission than an outside member, through a full member, but not among themselves. The commission for an outside member is £18 per lot round-turn (*i.e.* £9 in and £9 out). Deals opened and closed during the same day are at exactly half commission.

The workings of the market are much the same as those of the cocoa market already described. Business starts at 10.40 a.m., with each transaction being called over by the Chairman. There are further calls at 12.30 p.m., 3.30 p.m. and 4.45 p.m. In the intervening periods, business is conducted openly by members among themselves. After the close of the market, business goes on until the close of the US market with brokers trading among themselves from their own offices. This is known as "kerb trading" and business counts as being done for the next day. In the same way as with cocoa, all transactions are recorded and registered with the International Commodities Clearing House and this includes contracts struck on the kerb. The closing call is taken as the basis for the payment of margins to the Clearing House. However, each day, a Price Committee appointed by the United Terminal Market Association establishes what is known as the London Daily Price (commonly known as the LDP). This price represents the value of prompt-delivery raw sugar and is based on reported business in physical sugar or the tone of the futures market. This price is widely used as a price on which physical contracts are fixed as

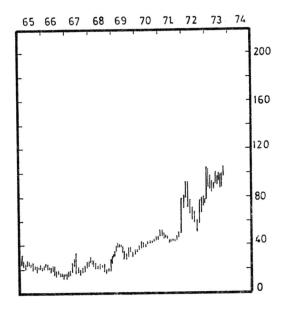

Fig. 4.2. Sugar: monthly range of spot prices, 1965–October 1973 (in £/long ton).

opposed to the price of the prompt month, which can be subject to technical squeeze.

If any month is bid over or offered over at more than £5 per ton from the previous day's 12.30-call closing buyer's price, trading halts in that month until there is a reverse of the situation, meaning that the pool of buyers' or sellers' orders is satisfied at the limit movement. Should this not happen, dealing in that month remains closed until the 2.30 call on the day following the 12.30 call from which the limit has been calculated.

There are also futures markets in New York and Paris. The New York market is roughly the same size as the London market and there is a large arbitrage business between the two. The Paris market is much smaller and the contract is for white refined sugar in contrast to the London and New York markets and this provides for a good basis for arbitrage. Over the years the sugar market has had some very good movements (*see* Fig. 4.2) but has never been as popular as the cocoa market with the less

Table 4.2. Sugar: London futures transactions, 1959–73 (in long tons)

Year	Transactions
1959 (Oct.–Dec.)	605,050
1960	1,148,900
1961	2,257,250
1962	3,967,300
1963	15,121,000
1964	13,092,900
1965	10,132,700
1966	8,602,300
1967	22,874,550
1968	19,777,850
1969	28,973,950
1970	26,543,500
1971	33,807,300
1972	43,951,000
1973	42,702,250

Source: International Commodities Clearing House Ltd

experienced speculator. This is probably because there are more complicated factors that affect the market, but this also makes it more popular with the professional. Taking all the commodity markets into account, both soft and hard, the sugar market is one of the "big four" and in the writer's own personal opinion one of the best in which to trade.

COFFEE

Background

Coffee is a commodity the origin of which goes back a long way and it was being mentioned as a drug by an Arabian physician as long ago as A.D. 900. It was later mentioned as a food, as a wine, and as having certain medicinal qualities such as being a remedy for the widely differing ailments of dropsy, gout and sore eyes. In the United Kingdom, the drink was at first thought of as a mildly stimulating drug. Today, coffee is one of the largest items in world trade after petroleum.

The coffee production cycle is an interesting one in that it is a cycle of years of shortage followed by even longer years of glut. At the end of the First World War, Brazil was the world's largest exporter of coffee—a position that it still holds today—and in the years between the wars production grew on average at a fast rate over the period. Production during the 1940s fell sharply, reflecting general world depression, frosts and drought, and the loss of the European markets because of the Second World War. After the war, Brazilian production expanded rapidly again, which created the need for an International Coffee Agreement to secure reasonable prices for producers. However, production again suffered a setback in the 1960s as a result of crop damage, although it has since improved again. The Brazilian cycle is to a large extent typical of the world cycle, although East Africa has boosted its share of the world market significantly over the period. Its share of exportable production in the 1930s was about 5 per cent, about 15 per cent in the 1950s and more than 25 per cent in the 1960s. It is from Africa that the United Kingdom obtains the bulk of its coffee, largely because of Commonwealth ties.

Coffee trees grow best in tropical regions of high altitude (2000 to 6000 feet above sea level) receiving a fair amount of rainfall. An average temperature of 18° to 21° Centigrade is ideal. Frost or drought can severely affect crops, whereas the right conditions can produce bumper yields. In Brazil coffee is grown mainly on fairly large estates, in contrast to Africa, where it is grown largely by smallholders. The coffee grown in Brazil is different from that grown in Africa and is of the Arabica variety in contrast to the African Robusta variety.

The market

A Coffee Trade Association was in existence in London as early as 1888, but the Coffee Terminal Market Association of London opened in July 1958 with a contract of 5 long tons of Uganda unwashed, native-grown Robusta coffee. All prices quoted are "in warehouse London, Liverpool or Bristol" and the Rules and Regulations of the Association allow the tender of a limited number of qualities below the official standard

Table 4.3. Coffee: London futures transactions,
1958–73 (in long tons)

Year	*Transactions*
1958 (July–Dec.)	53,935
1959	127,165
1960	115,180
1961	39,985
1962	26,650
1963	79,195
1964	315,555
1965	448,465
1966	325,180
1967	190,000
1968	190,000
1969	240,000
1970	375,685
1971	391,200
1972	301,705
1973	761,135

Source: International Commodities Clearing House Ltd

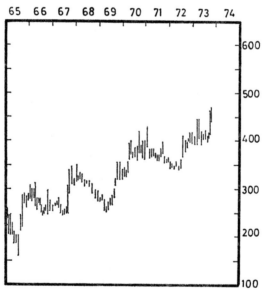

Fig. 4.3. Coffee: monthly range of spot prices,
1965–October 1973 (in £/long ton).

as well as Robusta coffee from most other countries, at differential prices
fixed by the Association. The contract is for up to twelve months forward
with the delivery months being January, March, May, July, September and
November. The market, like the cocoa market and the sugar market, is
housed in the Corn Exchange Building in Mark Lane, although all three
were until 1973 in Plantation House, Mincing Lane. Business commences
at 10.30 a.m. with a call, in the same way as with sugar and cocoa. There
are further calls at 12.30 p.m., 2.45 p.m. and a closing call at 4.50 p.m.
Contracts are guaranteed and cleared by the International Commodities
Clearing House.

The full members of the market are allowed to deal on the floor of the
exchange and associate members can deal at a lower rate of commission
than outsiders. The commission for an outsider is £14 per lot (£7 in,
£7 out).

In September 1973 a dollar contract in Arabica coffee was introduced.
The contract is for 5865 kg (or 85 bags of 69 kg) of sound wet processed
Arabica coffee ex warehouse approved by the Association in London,
Amsterdam, Rotterdam or Hamburg. Delivery is in the months of
February, April, June, August, October and December, up to thirteen
months forward. Further details of this contract, such as commission and
trading hours, may be found in Appendix 2.

The coffee market is the poor relation in terms of turnover to the sugar
and cocoa markets, as can be seen from Table 4.3 showing the volume of
business. There is no doubt this has in part been due to the success of the
International Coffee Agreement, suspended in September 1973, in keeping
prices stable. However, the chart of price movements shows that these have
not been insignificant and the market interests speculators who wish to
trade without the risk involved in the other more active markets. Should
coffee ever come into very short supply, the market has the potential to
become as active as those for cocoa and sugar.

WHEAT AND BARLEY

The London Grain Futures Market has been in existence since 1963.
Trading takes place across a ring on the Baltic Mercantile and Shipping
Exchange in their impressive building in St Mary Axe. Business is by
open outcry but is never conducted through a Chairman in contrast to
the other markets described in this chapter. The prices of all trades are
marked on a board by an official of the London Corn Trade Association,
who also enters the official opening and closing prices of each session.
These latter prices are fixed by a member nominated each week by the
Secretary of the Association, from a panel approved by the Council.

The market opens at 11.30 a.m. and closes at 12.45 p.m., reopening at 2.45 and finally closing at 4.15 p.m. Both wheat and barley are traded on the market and the contract is for 100 long tons (2240 lb) subject to certain conditions. Delivery of the wheat or barley is to be taken in a store approved by the Committee of the London Grain Futures Market within the counties authorised for the contract, and the grain is to be of a certain standard, as follows:

Wheat
1. The wheat is to be sound and sweet and to contain not more than 3 per cent heat damage.
2. The natural weight is to be not less than 58 lb per bushel.
3. The moisture content is not to exceed $15\frac{1}{2}$ per cent.
4. The total admixture of seeds and/or other farinaceous grains (including wild oats) and dirt is not to exceed 2 per cent, of which the dirt content is not to exceed 1 per cent. Ergot and/or garlic is not to exceed 0·001 per cent and sprouted grains 2 per cent.

Barley
1. The barley is to be sound and sweet and to contain not more than 3 per cent heat damage.
2. The natural weight is not to be less than 50 lb per bushel.
3. The moisture content is not to exceed $15\frac{1}{2}$ per cent.
4. The total admixture of seeds and/or farinaceous grains is not to exceed 5 per cent, of which the dirt content is not to exceed 1 per cent. Sprouted grains are not to exceed 5 per cent.

The price of the wheat or barley is to include insurance cover and free rent for fourteen days from the date of tender, and delivery is to be free to the buyers in bulk ex-store. At time of tender, the grain must be stored in the premises of an Approved Service Operator on the list authorised and published by the Council.

Trading is in the months of September, November, January, March and May, and so it is possible to deal only nine months forward. The number of months open for trading at any given time is subject to authorisation by the Council and only the months so authorised will appear on the board. Prices are quoted in pounds sterling per ton with the minimum fluctuation being £0·05. There is no daily limit as to how far prices may move.

The conduct of the market is under the control of the London Grain Futures Association, an association sponsored by the London Corn Trade Association, which has assumed responsibility for the organisation and running of the Clearing House. The executive body controlling the day-to-day business of the market is the London Grain Futures Council, which is composed of four elected members, six members appointed by the LCTA and two members appointed by the National Association of Corn and Agricultural Merchants, the President of the LCTA being *ex-officio* Chairman.

The LCTA holds a reserve fund which has been built up from an allotted portion of the Clearing House registration fees. The use of this fund is governed by an article in the LCTA constitution which permits, at any one time, up to 50 per cent of the fund to be used at the discretion of the Executive for settling claims by members arising out of the default of a member or the insolvency of a storekeeper.

Full members of the LGFA have to be members of the Baltic Mercantile and Shipping Exchange, members of the LCTA and owners of an LGFA certificate which can be obtained in the open market or purchased from the Association for £100.

Provision in the Articles is made for country membership, subscribers and subscriber brokers. The last two categories have to pay an annual subscription of £100. A special scale of reduced brokerages is contained in the bye-laws for all three categories.

A set of bye-laws has been drawn up by the Council of the LGFA, which has power to alter them. These bye-laws give the Council wide powers to control the activities of members, but any amendment to contract terms recommended by the Council has to be approved by the Executive of the LCTA and, of course, no such amendment will apply to contracts already made. The bye-laws contain a set of general regulations governing the conduct of the market, including powers to close the market on the declaration of an emergency, special regulations governing brokerages and special regulations governing margins.

Details of the volume of business on the market are not published, but since 1970 business has grown enormously as there has been less Government intervention in the physical market and grains have moved from being in gross over-supply to being in gross under-supply. The market is a viable one for the speculator, and, while he does not have the same flexibility as in some of the other soft commodity markets, he can generally do a fairly sizeable amount of business without moving the market against him. Although there is not a great deal of speculation outside the trade and many contracts are settled by delivering or taking delivery, this situation might well change in the future.

VEGETABLE OILS

The London Vegetable Oil Terminal Market opened in July 1967 and over a period of months three vegetable oil contracts for soyabean oil, coconut oil and sunflowerseed oil were introduced. These were unfortunately not a success and after some months the markets became dormant. During 1973 it was decided to resuscitate the soyabean oil contract and this was put into effect with the contract size being increased from 20 long tons to 50 tonnes. Other details of the contract are given in Appendix 2, but the contract specification is for crude degummed soyabean oil of the following standard:

FFA (as oleic–molec weight 282)	Max. 0·75 per cent
Moisture and volatile matter	Max. 0·20 per cent
Impurities (insoluble in petrol ether)	Max. 0·10 per cent
Lecithin (expressed as phosphorous)	Max. 0·02 per cent
Sediment (Gardner break test)	Max. 0·10 per cent
Colour (1″ Lovibond cell)	Max. 50 yellow + 5 red

Oil with a flashpoint below 121°C (250°F) is not tenderable.

It is unlikely that UK investors will be interested in this particular vegetable oil as the price is quoted in US dollars and cents and under exchange control regulations it is difficult for UK residents to trade in a dollar commodity. The reason for the change from sterling to dollars was to try to attract Continental interest which had previously been lacking, and it was felt that this was initially more important than attracting the UK private investor.

Initial reaction to the new soyabean contract was quite favourable and in January 1974 a new sterling contract for palm oil was instituted. This was also for 50 tonnes, but with the price in sterling. Other details of the contract are given in Appendix 2, but the contract specification is for crude unbleached palm oil of the following standard:

On arrival

Maximum percentage FFA (palmitic–molecular weight 256) acceptable for storage	4 per cent
Maximum percentage moisture and impurities acceptable for storage	0·5 per cent

On re-delivery

Maximum percentage FFA (palmitic–molecular weight 256) guaranteed by the Tank Installation	6 per cent
Maximum percentage moisture and impurities guaranteed by the Tank Installation	0·75 per cent

The price is basis 5 per cent FAA and basis purity, with premiums and discounts based on out-turn.

Palm oil has been one of the great successes since the early 1960s with tremendous increases in production, particularly from Malaysia, and with world demand keeping up with the increase in production. It is anticipated

that private investors may find this contract to be of interest and certainly
it is one that should be watched in view of continual demand and possible
volatility of supply.

WOOL

The London Wool Terminal Market was one of the first markets to open
again after the Second World War and it did so in April 1953. The contract
is for 2250 kg standard top which shall be made from merino wool,
grown and shorn from living animals in Australia. It shall be dry-combed
and contain the standard allowance of grease and oil. The wool is to be
sorted and scoured, carded and combed in accordance with the methods
prevailing in the wool textile industry. The specifications of the standard
are as follows:

Fibre fineness as expressed by the WIRA Fibre Fineness Meter 22·5 microns.

Fibre length as expressed by the Almeter:

Hauteur	6·2 cm
Barbe	7·7 cm
Coefficient of variation of hauteur	50 per cent

Most contracts are closed out before maturity, although about 2 per cent
of all contracts result in physical deliveries. Tenders must be made to the

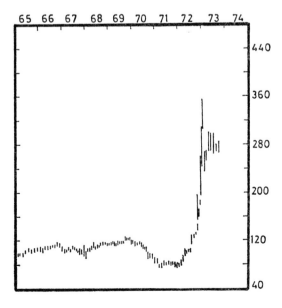

Fig. 4.4. Wooltops: monthly range of spot prices, 1965–October 1973 (in pence/kg).

Clearing House by 3.00 p.m. on any business day up to and including the last working day of the month of delivery. Each tender, including re-tenders, must specify the contract it represents, state the price and be accompanied by an Appraisal Certificate, a Conditioning House Certificate for moisture and fatty matter, Test Certificates for micron and length, and a Warehouseman's Warrant. The buyer will pay to the seller through the Clearing House, as agent, a fee of £5 in respect of each lot tendered to him.

The contract is for up to nineteen months ahead with the delivery months being March, May, July, October and December. Trading takes place between 11.15 and 11.30 a.m., 3.15 and 3.30 p.m., and 4.15 and 4.45 p.m. Kerb trading is allowed after hours until 5.30 p.m. but contracts must be telephoned to the Clearing House by 5.45 p.m. All contracts on the market must be registered with the International Commodities Clearing House. The Clearing House guarantees the fulfilment of the contract to the person in whose name it is registered in accordance with its rules and those of the

Table 4.4. Wool: London futures transactions,
1953–73 (in '000 lb)

Year	Transactions
1953 (May–Dec.)	34,695
1954	95,045
1955	73,100
1956	108,755
1957	184,780
1958	202,885
1959	281,850
1960	269,540
1961	265,780
1962	149,090
1963	238,235
1964	233,550
1965	162,970
1966	121,700
1967	140,000
1968	95,000
1969	40,000
1970	26,590
1971	15,520
1972	21,180
1973	18,680

Source: International Commodities Clearing House Ltd

Association. Membership of the market is divided into three categories: floor membership, affiliate membership and associate membership. The commission for a non-member is £9 per lot buying and £9 per lot selling.

From Table 4.4 showing the amount of transactions on the market, it can be seen that the volume of business has dropped quite dramatically in recent years. This is due mainly to the competition wool has received from synthetic fibres and to the fact that there is a more attractive contract on the Sydney market for producers and consumers. It is against the Bank of England exchange control regulations for the private investor in the United Kingdom to use the Sydney market, and the volume of business on the London market has dropped to such an extent that it is now sometimes difficult for even a small investor to get in and out of the market without moving the prices a disproportionate amount against himself. However, all futures markets go through periods of great activity and inactivity and this market may have its day again.

TEA

All the soft commodities that have futures markets have now been discussed, but there are many other soft commodities in which a private investor might wish to invest. In any of these he would have to buy the commodity at source or at auction and store it and pay rent and insurance. He would not be able to deal in a small amount and would in all probability find it difficult to sell when he wanted to. For this reason, there is little outside interest in commodities that do not have futures markets.

It is, however, perhaps worth describing the process of sale of one commodity that is typical of other commodities that do not have a futures market as it will illustrate the difficulties that a private investor would have should he wish to become involved. Tea is a good example, as the United Kingdom consumes nearly 40 per cent of the world's exports of this commodity.

When tea has been harvested and processed on a tea estate, it is packed into plywood chests lined with aluminium foil to keep it fresh and sent to the local ports for export, unless it has been privately sold or is sent to local auctions. All the chests of a particular grade coming from one estate at one time are called a "break". After having arrived at a warehouse in the United Kingdom 2 kilos of tea are taken from one chest from each break and are distributed as samples for examination by the brokers who are going to sell the tea and those who are going to buy it. A selling broker acts on behalf of the producer and the tea distributors purchase through a buying broker.

The brokers taste and advise on the quality of the tea and its value, and deal with the documents of title, from the time the tea leaves the country of origin to the time it has been bought by the distributors. Selling brokers prepare lists of tea for sale for prospective buyers, and these prospective buyers and the buying brokers acting for them draw samples from the warehouse through the tea clearing house (which also deals with and distributes the documents of title). When the prospective buyers have tasted and valued the samples, they are able to decide whether to buy the quantity offered at the auction. Most of the tea arriving in the United Kingdom is sold at auction at the new Tea Trade Centre in Sir John Lyon House in the City.

After the tea has been purchased, weight notes and warrants are sent to the buyers showing full particulars of the lots: the name and address of the warehouse where the tea is stored; the name of the estate; the name of the ship which imported the tea; the gross weight of tea and the net weight of each chest; and the grade of tea. These documents give buyers authority to remove their tea from the original warehouse. The tea can stay in the warehouse indefinitely, but the buyers have to pay rent two months after the purchase date, or it is removed to private warehouses where it is stored until required. A private speculator would not be able to get involved in this process unless he was doing it through an expert connected with the trade, and such experts are unlikely to be interested in speculative business unless it is on a large scale. The process for other soft commodities without a futures market is not exactly the same but is on the whole as complicated.

One of the advantages of commodity trading is that it is not possible to deal with thousands of different commodites and so a speculator can soon become relatively expert in the markets available. In the soft commodities each year brings a new crop and with it an exciting and challenging new investment possibility.

Chapter 5

Rubber, Metals and Bullion

Rubber

T. S. E. FIGGIS
Director, S. Figgis & Co. Ltd

General

Whether growing as a wild plant in the tropical jungles of Brazil or in the rows of orderly trees in a modern plantation in Malaysia there is a romantic flavour in the story of rubber which few major commodities can equal.

Originally rubber was collected wild in South America and Africa, but as a result of the smuggling of seeds of the tree *Hevea Brasiliensis* to Kew Gardens and the despatch of seedlings later to the Botanical Gardens in Colombo and Singapore the plantation industry in the East expanded very quickly, and soon became the main source of the supplies of natural rubber.

While this was happening on one side of the world, the motor-car industry, revolutionised by the invention of the pneumatic tyre by John Boyd Dunlop, was expanding equally fast on the other.

Production

Malaysia is the foremost producer of natural rubber, both in the quantity produced and in the sophisticated research and development on which both the Malaysian Government and the large plantation groups spend much money and effort.

Of latter years much has also been done to improve the quality of the rubber produced by the thousands of smallholders, much of whose production has in the past been of low quality. In Indonesia, where large estates under British and Dutch control were originally established, political difficulties and unrest prevented for a number of years the same sort of development as has taken place in Malaysia, but under the present stable government conditions are improving.

Vietnam, Cambodia and Ceylon in the East, and Nigeria in West Africa, are the other principal producers.

Consumption

The large tyre-making companies, either American, British, French, Italian or German, are among the best-known names in international industry. Tyres, however, account for only part of the natural rubber consumed, and the number of individual users for all manner of rubber goods is legion.

In order to provide all these potential purchasers with their requirements at the right time, in the right place, and with the right grade, the present marketing system has grown up.

It would not be possible to describe any particular pattern which manufacturers follow in purchasing their requirements. Some may make a practice of being well covered for some months ahead, others prefer to buy on a hand-to-mouth basis, and all consumers will be influenced by the ruling level of prices.

It may, however, be said that since the holding of stocks in consuming areas became less remunerative, owing to the immensely high cost of finance and warehousing, consumers have to be prepared to be covered in their requirements further ahead than when they were able to rely on replenishing from spot goods.

One of the features of the rubber industry is the development by some of the largest consumers of their own plantations. Dunlop has for many years had its own plantations in Malaysia, while most of the larger American companies have done the same, the most notable perhaps being Firestone in Liberia. This does not mean, however, that these companies are able to supply all their own requirements, and it is safe to say that all of them have come to the market sooner or later to obtain their supplies.

Grades

Space does not permit a full account of all developments, even those since the early 1960s. It must be sufficient to state that in the early years rubber was produced in the form of Ribbed Smoked Sheets, the quality of which was judged on its cleanliness, and Pale or Brown Crêpes, the value of which depended on cleanliness and colour.

Beginning in the early 1960s, in order to meet the threat of synthetic rubber taking a still larger share of the market, and to improve the general presentation of natural rubber, the Malaysian Government led the way in the development of a new product called Standard Malaysian Rubbers, the advantages of which are that the process within the factory can be shortened while quality is judged not by visual inspection but by laboratory specifications, strictly adhered to. The introduction of SMRs has also brought improvements in packing, leading to easier handling.

The success of this enterprise is shown by the growth of production of SMRs to nearly 426,000 tons in the twelve months ending in July 1973 out of a total production in Malaysia of about 1,400,000 tons, and by all the major producing countries following with a similar product.

Ribbed Smoked Sheet No. 1, however, still remains the grade used for hedging facilities, whether in London, Kuala Lumpur or Singapore.

Organised markets for the purchase and sale of rubber exist in Singapore, Kuala Lumpur, London and New York. Amsterdam, Paris and Hamburg all contain a number of firms actively engaged in the trade, but the details which follow refer only to the London market.

The market

The Rubber Trade Association of London was founded in 1913 and has controlled the trade in rubber in the United Kingdom, and to some extent elsewhere because of the wide acceptance of its contracts, ever since. Clearly many changes have taken place since 1913, but throughout this period every effort has been made to keep abreast of all worthwhile developments.

The Association is composed of three classes of members, Importers and Producers, Brokers, and Dealers, and in 1973 their numbers were fifty, ten and thirty-one respectively. There are also thirty-eight associate members from all over the world, whereas full membership is restricted to firms domiciled in the United Kingdom. Of the Association's many responsibilities and functions the drafting of contracts and arbitration arrangements are the most important.

London is an international market in the broadest sense, and business is transacted daily to a large number of destinations all over the world. There is close contact on the one hand with the Eastern markets in Kuala Lumpur and Singapore, and on the other with consumers everywhere, especially in Europe, as well as government agencies and other buyers in the Eastern bloc. The main business transacted is in one of the Sheet grades ranging from RSS 1 to RSS 5, or in one of the newer Comminuted or Crumb Rubbers (SMRs) gradually superseding the more traditional grades. There are, however, a number of other grades produced from the latex which flows from the tree, and, whether it is the cleanest and purest, collected daily or several times a week, down to the semi-coagulated lump and scrap which can be recovered from the tree or from the installations in the estate factory, very little indeed is wasted and all of it can be used.

No figures are published of the tonnage traded in physical rubber in London, but it seems probable that the quantity is greater today than ever before.

Most business in physical rubber is traded on either the Eastern f.o.b. contract or the London c.i.f. contracts, the latter being widely used by both producers and consumers.

In days gone by, there were a large number of official grades of rubber, eventually standardised to some extent in the Green Book of the International Rubber Quality and Packing Conference. The introduction of Standard Malaysian Rubbers was intended to provide manufacturers with a much smaller but acceptable choice based on scientific formulae, and this has indeed happened, although perhaps to a smaller extent than hoped for.

Reference was made above to Ribbed Smoked Sheet No. 1 as the grade used for hedging purposes, and this is perhaps the place to refer to these facilities.

The futures market in London, where rubber can be bought and sold for delivery (rather than shipment on c.i.f. terms), is based on a contract organised by the Rubber Settlement House. This is a broker's contract, settlements taking place at least once in two weeks, and more often when fluctuations are rapid.

The contract is based on three-month quarterly periods (*i.e.* January–March, April–June, etc.), although single months may also be dealt in. The minimum quantity is 5 tons for each single month, 15 tons for a normal three-month period.

Rubber is unusual to the extent that trading is permitted up to three years ahead, which concession offers a wide variety of premiums and discounts over the spot position. Whether the fullest use has been made in the past of these hedging facilities is certainly open to doubt. There are, however, reasons for this. One is that some producers are willing to make forward sales of their production to a greater extent than in most other commodities and have less need therefore to avail themselves of the hedging market. Another reason is that the physical market in RSS 1 is often used as a hedging medium instead of the more normal delivery contract. However, recently a much larger business has been transacted daily, and 1973 accounted for the largest yet recorded.

The Rubber Settlement House contract has now been in existence without material change for over fifty years. However, in December 1973 the Rubber Trade Association agreed in principle to change over to a contract covered by the International Commodities Clearing House, which will operate from late 1974 or early 1975.

In the early days of large-scale dealing in rubber, in the years from 1918 to about 1930, rubber was with cotton probably the most popular speculative medium among commodities. A great deal of money was made, and lost, in the boom years of 1924, 1925 and 1926.

In 1931 and 1932, when Europe and the United States were hit by an economic blizzard which brought President Roosevelt to office, rubber slumped to such a low level that the plantation industry nearly died. The price did in fact decline for a short time to less than 2*d* per lb (or 1·836p per kg).

With the price now standing at around 45p per kg producers are certainly not in a position to complain. The more far-sighted among them probably would feel more comfortable if the price to the consumer was somewhat less.

During the Second World War, when the supply of natural rubber was almost entirely cut off by the Japanese occupation of the Eastern producing areas, the United States developed of necessity its production of synthetic rubber from oil, a process which had been already known but not developed until the need arose.

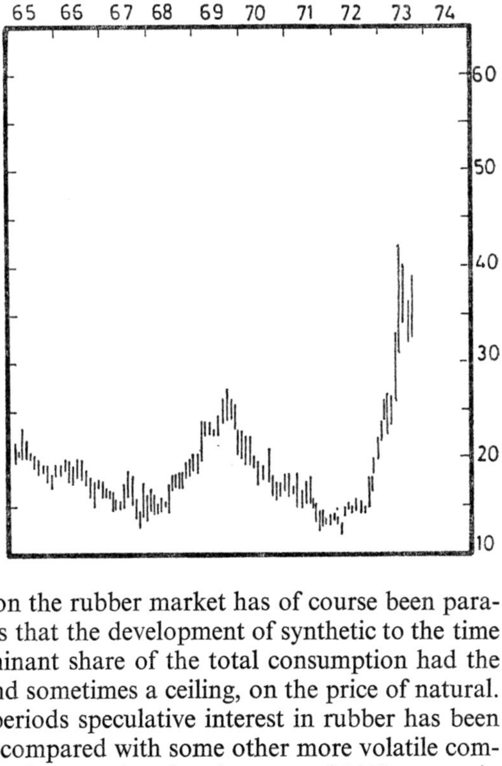

Fig. 5.1. Rubber: monthly range of spot prices, 1965–October 1973 (in pence/kg).

The impact of synthetic on the rubber market has of course been paramount, but the point here is that the development of synthetic to the time when it obtained a predominant share of the total consumption had the effect of putting a brake, and sometimes a ceiling, on the price of natural.

Consequently, for long periods speculative interest in rubber has been small, and in no way to be compared with some other more volatile commodities. There is, however, always a time for change, and 1973, a year in which nearly all commodities were in enormous demand, brought a considerable speculative interest into the market.

Synthetic rubber
For many years the synthetic rubber industry was regarded by the producers of natural rubber as Enemy No. 1 whose main object seemed to be to capture the whole of the consumer trade. In the last few years an identity

of interest has materialised and there is now a much closer concern with
the trade as a whole, due at least in part to the knowledge that both types
of rubber are in demand for certain end-uses, and that the middle ground
is the only territory where conflict is likely to arise.

In all the major consuming countries the proportion of synthetic
rubber used is much greater than of natural rubber. Since all the natural
rubber produced is sold, it is clear that without the advent of synthetic
the world as we know it would have come nearly to a standstill.

In the United States, the largest consumer of rubber, 650,679 tons of
natural were used in 1972 and 2,328,279 tons of synthetic. In the United
Kingdom the figures were 174,000 tons of natural against 272,600 tons of
synthetic.

Apart altogether from the suitability to the consumer of either type of
rubber, synthetic has one enormous advantage in its ready availability,
since in most cases it is produced in the same country, or near to it, as its
consumption.

Whereas natural rubber has to overcome the disadvantage of a long sea
journey, with its expensive freight and vulnerability to delay, synthetic can
in normal times be supplied to order within a short time, possibly a few
days, and be delivered straight into the buyer's factory.

In order to counterbalance these advantages natural-rubber producers
have made great efforts to maintain supplies at regular intervals, overcom-
ing in the process the uncertain effects of a tropical climate, rising freight
rates and a latterly much reduced shipping service. However, recently a
new factor has appeared in the shape of the threatened world shortage of
oil, clearly a real threat to supplies of an article dependent on oil for its
existence. The future of the whole rubber industry depends to a large
extent on how this threat develops.

Metals and Bullion

R. GIBSON-JARVIE
Executive Secretary, The London Metal Exchange

THE LONDON METAL EXCHANGE

The LME stands in many ways somewhat apart from the other London
commodity markets, being in several important respects different both as
to its constitution and as to its method of operation. Like its neighbours

in the City, the Metal Exchange originated as a forum where the London merchants could meet and trade among themselves by open outcry. The precise date of its origin is not clear, but records show it as a formal market by the year 1876. The Metal Market and Exchange Company was incorporated in 1881, and the LME still occupies the building in Whittington Avenue into which it moved in 1882.

Membership of the Exchange is personal, and may be either as an Individual Subscriber—originally one who traded on his own account—or as the Representative Subscriber nominated by a company or firm to trade on its behalf. The companies which are thus represented on the Exchange are a cross-section of the metals industry worldwide. Apart from producers and consumers trading either in their own names or through a market company set up for the purpose, there is a strong leavening of members conducting a more generalised clients' business. There do exist certain stipulations as to the UK registration of member companies, primarily in order to ensure that all are subject to UK taxation and commercial legislation, but these do not stand in the way of participation by overseas interests. Among the thirty Ring members now on the LME there are, for example, representatives of the United States, Canada, France, Germany, Holland, India and Japan—the last-named having now emerged as an important figure on the world metals scene. There are in addition some sixty "non-Ring" or associate members, who trade via those in the Ring.

A club, then? In a sense this might be said, since the LME has a relatively small membership, for which its requirements are somewhat eclectic. However, the significance of this lies in the factor which undoubtedly constitutes the main difference between the LME and the other commodity markets. All LME trading is on a principal's contract, and members so trading must therefore stand behind their market obligations as principals to them. *There is no clearing house, nor any clearing house guarantee.*

A further point of difference lies in the fact that, by futures market standards, a high proportion of physical business is transacted on the LME, and it is worth noting that not less than some 12 to 15 per cent of LME transactions do in fact run to maturity and result in the movement of metal into or out of warehouse. It is therefore quite true to say that the LME, in the persons of those who trade there, is geared at least as much to dealing in the metals *per se* as to the financial positions arising from such dealing. This does not of course exclude hedging, pricing, options trading or any of the other functions of a futures market. Indeed, the remoteness and in some cases the instability of many of the sources of supply makes the hedging of a forward sale or purchase a vital operation. Since it takes two to make a bargain, this in no way rules out, nor should it discourage, the

private investor whose main interest is financial and who is and remains
an essential "other leg" to so many of these market operations.

The contracts and the metals

The LME trades in four of the base non-ferrous metals: copper, tin, lead
and zinc. There is also a market in silver which runs in parallel with dealings
on the London Silver Market, and the possibility of extending the LME's
range is always under review. It is important to bear in mind that the
metals traded on the LME are all international both as to origin and as to
end-use, and that market prices are quoted in sterling—with all that that
implies in terms of currency and foreign exchange considerations.

The market in copper is the largest in terms of turnover, and to some
extent copper has come to be looked on by the investor as the standard
"chip" on the LME. This should not be taken so as to overshadow the
other metals when considering an investment: although perhaps the tin
market is somewhat specialised. As a guide to the sort of turnovers achieved
on the LME, that for copper in 1972 was 2,509,750 tonnes, and in 1973 to
the end of June was already 2,413,825 tonnes. Trading in copper and tin
are both as old as the Exchange itself, while the other metals have been
introduced at various dates since: the silver market was in fact re-started
as recently as 1968, after a period of trading in the 1930s.

Official market dealings take place twice daily, commencing at noon
and again at 3.35 p.m., and each metal is traded for two five-minute Rings

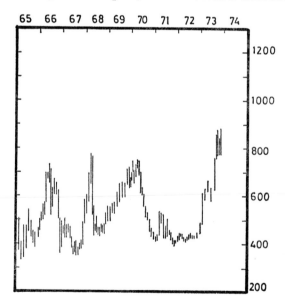

Fig. 5.2. Copper:
monthly range of spot
prices, 1965–October
1973 (in £/tonne).

in each session. There is a period of informal "kerb" trading after the end of each of the two official sessions, when all five metals are traded simultaneously. To one unused to the spectacle, Ring trading has most of the apparent attributes of Bedlam; in fact it is remarkably easy, after some experience, to follow what is taking place. Certainly, no more effective method of bringing buyers and sellers together and for them rapidly and conclusively to arrive at meaningful prices has yet been evolved. Since the first official session does not begin until noon, a considerable amount of "pre-market" trading by telephone is done beforehand; a client may, however, instruct the member acting for him to disregard this, and trade on his behalf only in the Ring.

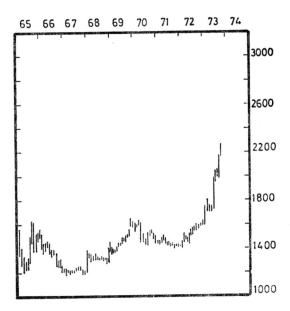

Fig. 5.3. Tin: monthly range of spot prices, 1965–October 1973 (in £/tonne).

The Official Prices are arrived at during the second five-minute Ring for each metal in the noon session, with figures for cash and three-months buyers and sellers announced, as well as further seven-months prices for silver. (Incidentally, there are no limits on the LME such as exist on certain other markets as to any permitted range of price movements during one day, or one market session.) The prices are assessed by a Quotations Committee consisting of three senior dealers in the Ring, who take on this task in rotation for two weeks at a time. They are announced after the final Ring of the noon session and are forthwith transmitted by Reuters worldwide, to stand as the point of reference for virtually all trade in those metals for the ensuing twenty-four hours. (Note that these daily "prompts" are another point of difference between the LME and most other markets.)

It is most important to appreciate how the LME "Settlement Price" (cash sellers) performs this essential function, even—or perhaps especially—in respect of direct producer-to-consumer business not necessarily done on the LME at all. This is perhaps the Exchange's most vital function, in that it thus provides a free-market price arrived at by open dealings, for use by industry the world over.

The LME fixes its own requirements as to the grades and shapes of all metals save copper, which must conform either to those of the British Standards Institution or the American Society for Testing Materials; and there are definite requirements which have to be met before a metal brand is registered as a good delivery on the market. There are in fact two copper contracts—for cathodes and for wirebars—of which the latter is the larger market at the present time, and usually trades at a premium over cathodes.

With the Exchange thus physically oriented, and since the contracts stipulate delivery in warehouse (location at the seller's option), a number of delivery points have been registered over the years, both in the United Kingdom and at Antwerp, Rotterdam and Hamburg as well. To date, Antwerp and Hamburg are registered for copper and tin, although a certain amount of silver is stored also in Hamburg. (As a general rule,

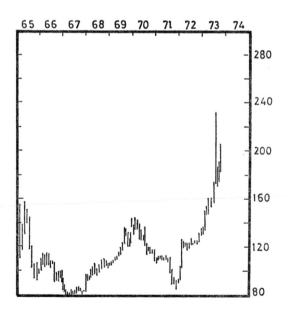

Fig. 5.4. Lead: monthly range of spot prices, 1965–October 1973 (in £/tonne).

silver is stored in bank vaults.) For anyone seriously contemplating investment on the LME, it is important to have some insight into the significance of warehouse stocks. All LME contracts are backed by metal on warrant and the amount of material in stock at any time is a factor in market pricing. Not that these amounts in any way limit turnover, since under a forward contract it is possible for the same parcel to be bought and sold many times over before eventually being taken out of warehouse and into use. High prices and turnovers in conjunction with low or falling stocks may cause, or increase the extent of, a backwardation—a premium of

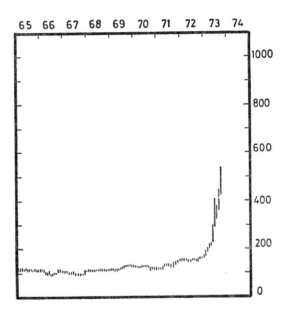

Fig. 5.5. Zinc: monthly range of spot prices, 1965–October 1973 (in £/tonne).

cash or nearby metal over the more remote dates. The extent of the "back" will very largely depend on supply conditions, and the likelihood either of fresh material coming forward to replenish existing stocks or of further demands being made on them.

Conversely, high or increasing stocks in warehouse would normally be associated with a contango—a premium of three months over cash, and for the most part representing the finance cost to the holder of carrying stocks for the period. In a contango situation it is possible for anyone or any institution having surplus cash, or access to cheap funds, to "borrow"— *i.e.* to buy cash and sell forward in one operation. In this way, he will make the difference between the full amount of the contango and the net cost of finance to himself. This is an important factor in the financing of heavy stocks overhanging the market, as was the case during the greater part of 1971 and 1972.

The minimum trading lots for each of the metals are: for copper, lead and zinc 25 tonnes, for tin 5 tonnes and for silver 10,000 troy ounces. They are represented by warehouse warrants for these amounts, with a permitted tolerance of 2 per cent either side in actual weight. Set against current or recent prices, therefore, it can be seen that the Metal Exchange is a market where anyone operating must stand ready to do so in fairly significant figures.

Trading rules and commissions
There is no hard-and-fast rule on the LME as to deposits or margins, such as exists on those exchanges whose contracts are registered with the International Commodities Clearing House, or on Comex in New York (whence, incidentally, much arbitrage business emanates in copper and silver). An initial deposit will as a rule be required by the LME member acting for a client and 10 per cent could be taken as average. Save in silver dealings on the LME, where they are mandatory, margins need not necessarily be called during the course of a transaction, although there is a clause in the contracts for this to be done at discretion. (Note that, under the LME principal's contract, if margins are called it will be the member himself and not the Exchange or a clearing house which will do so.)

Commissions on the LME are another of the points of difference between it and the other commodity markets and the Stock Exchange. On the LME there is no set scale, and members may charge what they see fit. Again as a generalisation, it would be unlikely for a client to be asked for more than a quarter per cent of an opening purchase. In fact, the LME contracts are so worded that any percentage is expressed not as a commission but as a part of the price. This stood the Exchange in good stead where VAT was concerned, since all transactions where one of the parties is an LME member, and which do not result in delivery of metal out of warehouse (save for export), are zero rated for VAT. Being expressed as part of the price therefore, any percentage is similarly treated.

For the private investor: a word of caution
Although in no sense dominated by any one sector of the metal market, the LME is geared more to physical trading than the other exchanges. It follows from this that a private investor should have a passable knowledge of supply and demand conditions governing metals, as well as be aware of any currency or other technical considerations which might be manifest at any time. It is also true that the LME moves generally in longer and somewhat less pronounced cycles than do the markets in the soft commodities: flurries of speculative activity can and do occur, but it is often

wiser for him to allow each of these to run its course before establishing
or modifying his own position. To do this successfully requires reserves—
not only of finance, but of courage!

THE LONDON BULLION MARKETS

If the Metal Exchange differs in many respects from the other London
commodity exchanges, the gold and silver markets stand even farther
apart from the rest. Neither the London Gold Market nor the London
Silver Market in fact has the same formalised constitution as do the LME
and the Mark Lane exchanges, and the membership is very strictly
limited. They consist of a small nucleus of companies trading in the two
metals.

The London Gold Market

The membership of the Gold Market is made up of five companies, who
meet twice daily to "fix" the price of gold—this is quoted in US dollars
per ounce, and in sterling. While the fixing is in progress, the offices of the
members are in touch with the outside world and the price is established
by matching supply and demand.

In the case of gold, it is of significance to the private investor in the
United Kingdom mainly as a key to the prices both of money and of other
commodities in relation to money. It is not permitted for a private individual
in the United Kingdom to hold or to trade in gold on his own account.
Thus, the prices arrived at in each day's fixing are a reference point for the
international trading which is carried on with other centres. The mystique
and the very real significance of gold still persist, and still affect world
trade in virtually every sphere of activity. Although no longer the official
common denominator of currency values, the huge premium of the free-
market price over the official one is in itself indicative of the continuing
influence of gold, and of the depreciation of the purchasing power of most
of the world's currencies in the face of widespread inflation.

The price of gold is not only relevant in this indirect way, however, and
there is a considerable physical market—in the fields of jewellery and
watchmaking as well as in electronics, chemistry and surgery, where the
virtual immutability of the metal has special virtues.

The companies which currently make up the Gold Market are Mocatta
& Goldsmid, N. M. Rothschild, Samuel Montagu, Sharps Pixley and
Johnson Matthey.

The London Silver Market

The LSM is open to the investor, since there are no governmental or
other barriers to inhibit trade in silver at commercial or individual level

64 *Trading in commodities*

in the United Kingdom. It is therefore worth while to examine the history, structure and mechanics of the LSM in a little more detail.

The London firms of Mocatta & Goldsmid, Pixley & Abell and Sharps & Wilkins, who had been trading in precious metals during the eighteenth and nineteenth centuries, started a weekly silver fixing during the 1880s. Although these fixings took place only once each week, there was daily trading in between based on these prices. At or about the beginning of the present century a daily fixing was instituted to fix spot and forward prices. In 1900 Samuel Montagu joined as a member; in 1957 Mocatta & Goldsmid were incorporated in the Hambros Bank Group and the two other original members merged to form Sharps Pixley Ltd. This company was taken over by the Kleinwort Benson group in 1963.

Besides the LSM and the LME the two other members of the Gold Market, N. M. Rothschild and Johnson Matthey, are active dealers in silver and the authorities have recognised this group as constituting the market for VAT purposes. The same degree of protection from the effects of VAT in dealings which do not result in actual delivery therefore covers both markets, as well as trade between them.

The silver fixing now takes place daily at 12.15, when spot, three months, six months and twelve months are quoted.

In its earlier years, the LSM conducted a predominantly entrepôt business, between producers in the western hemisphere and buyers for the most part in India and China. There was additionally a leavening of the

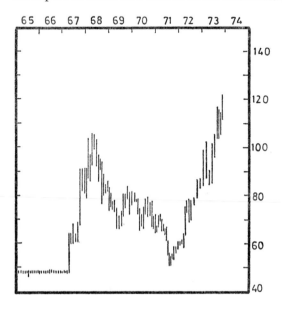

Fig. 5.6. Silver: monthly range of spot prices, 1965–October 1973 (in pence/troy oz).

speculative business for clients which brings such an important degree of flexibility to any commodity futures market. During these early days, and indeed until after the Second World War and the subsequent demonetisation of silver, the LSM was inevitably caught up in governmental decisions and changes of policy (not always either predictable or altogether reasonable) which could—and did—have disturbing effects on prices and trends.

With the New Deal programme during the first Roosevelt administration which began in 1933, a considerable amount of silver legislation was incorporated to help the silver producers in the United States. This raised the price from its depressed levels and silver flowed from the Far East to the United States. This had the effect of China having to abandon the silver standard. The policy was changed to buy only US domestically mined silver after about eighteen months. During this period a special silver profits tax was imposed. As a result silver was not traded on the New York Commodity Exchange until this tax was removed. The US Treasury thus accumulated large quantities of silver.

After the Second World War, many new uses for silver were found by industry, particularly in electronics and electrical contacts, besides the increased use in photography. As a result demand considerably exceeded new production even when supplemented by sporadic releases of hoarded metal, and the balance was sold by the US Treasury at a fixed price. The "free stocks" of the United States were exhausted in 1961, but it was decided to sell the silver backing of the silver certificates: as a result the Treasury kept the price of $1·29 per ounce until May 1967. At the same time the US silver coinage has gone out of circulation, being replaced by cupro-nickel "sandwich" coins.

With the US stocks no longer supporting the supply sources, and with industrial demand continuing—notably in electronics and the more sophisticated items of weaponry and space travel—the long-term trend of the silver market could be assumed to be in the main bullish. However, the metal's undoubted popularity as a hedge against currency fluctuations, not only short-term but as an "investment" by hoarders, can have some quite sharp and appreciable effects on any such overall trend.

With supplies limited as they are, it only requires a moderate flight out of currency on the one hand, or the release of a hoard on the other, to cause more than just a ripple in the prices both of spot and forward.

Chapter 6

Basic Guidelines for Successful Trading

P. LYNCH-GARBETT

Director, Bache & Co. (London) Ltd

INTRODUCTION

As we have learnt in earlier chapters that, similar to the Stock Exchange, access into trading in commodity futures markets is through the medium of a broker, then it becomes obvious that the investor needs firstly to communicate with a broker and secondly to become acquainted with him. A list of brokers is normally available from the Secretary of the Association of each commodity exchange. As it is an axiom of a competent broker to "know your client", so it should be a general principle of the investor to know his broker.

There are two broad classifications of traders in commodity futures:

1. Businessmen or firms who produce or market or process commodities. They protect the value of their physical stocks and of their forward sales commitments by engaging in offsetting futures transactions, thus eliminating or reducing the possibility of adverse world or local price movement, which is ever present. This protective procedure is called hedging and is dealt with in more detail in Chapters 3 and 8.
2. The private investor or speculator who voluntarily risks his capital with the expectation of making profits.

Both groups are essential ingredients of a successful commodity futures market, and, when it is generally known that the purpose of futures markets is to remove or reduce price risks in the process of marketing goods in a free capitalistic system, then it also can be accepted that the speculator is providing an important economic function in absorbing part of the risks which industry seeks to avoid.

There is no mystique about commodity trading. Although in some ways akin to trading in stocks and shares, trading in the futures markets is simplicity itself. There is no involvement with rights issues, ex-dividend dates, preferential votes, etc.; nor are there difficulties in selling short. This, however, does not imply that successful results in commodity trading are more certain.

A successful commodity trading programme comprises two basic components:

1. A knowledge of how to make the best use of available trading capital.
2. An ability to diagnose the markets correctly.

The first component—capital management—is far easier to master than the second, but, oddly, its proper use seems to be far less prevalent among non-professional commodity traders and is worth discussing at some length.

CAPITAL MANAGEMENT

Often an amateur trader will make only one or two really poor market judgements in the course of twenty or thirty trades and yet lose a major portion of his trading capital. Other traders might add up their total commissions at the end of the year and be startled to discover that they paid two or three times as much as their average account size while barely breaking even. These and other similar experiences result from poor, or non-existent, money management techniques and can be eliminated with a little planning and self-discipline.

Deciding on a capital commitment

Since commodity futures trading can be a highly speculative undertaking, it is important to determine in advance how much risk capital can be committed. This amount should be segregated from other assets, either in a futures trading account, or, perhaps, in a separate interest-bearing account from which funds may be withdrawn as the need for margin arises. Setting aside a speculative sum for the futures markets not only provides a known basis on which trading programmes can be built but also helps guard against the tendency to over-trade. The speculative amount that should be set aside for trading will naturally vary widely from person to person. Formulae based on income, net worth and asset liquidity do not take into account vital factors such as age, temperament and future goals, all of which should be considered before making a commitment. The best general guideline that can be given is that futures capital should be an amount which can be risked without endangering your peace of mind or lost without harming your financial position.

Maximum risk and minimum objective

One of the most basic rules for success in any venture is to plan what you are going to do before you do it. This elementary piece of common sense applies to commodity trading as much as to anything else. Although the volatility of futures prices demands that traders maintain flexibility, there are two views that should be ascertained in advance—your maximum risk and your minimum objective. Your maximum risk can be protected by the means of stop-loss orders, the timing of which can be discussed with the broker. The minimum objective is flexible and can be reduced upward or downward as subsequent developments and market action dictate. The initial stop-loss protection on the other hand should never be moved to allow greater risk. The whole purpose of a "stop" is to limit possible losses to predetermined levels, and, the closer a market gets to your "stop", the more likely it becomes that you have made an error in market judgement. It is perfectly acceptable, on the other hand, to move a "stop" nearer to the market price as a means of protecting profits against trend changes. The use of a profit objective is desirable because many traders have a marked tendency either quickly to take small profits or simply to let their profits erode until they turn into losses.

The wise trader will never put himself in the position of having to decide under stress whether to close out his losing position. His well-thought-out pre-established "stop" should take care of this contingency for him.

In assessing a market it is important to be sure that the Net potential profit/Potential loss ratio is at least 2:1. This really is justified by the fact that commodity prices tend to exhibit more sustained trends than would be expected on the basis of pure chance. This means that it is, on the whole, less than twice as difficult to take advantage of 200-point moves than 100-point moves, 50-point moves than 25-point moves, and so forth. It is worth mentioning that the psychological desirability of risking less than your expected reward does not, by itself, justify the use of a High reward/Risk ratio. This justification comes from the fact that sustained price movements in most futures markets occur in greater frequency than pure chance would predict. Discovering and taking advantage of such asymmetries is the key to profitable trading.

Limiting the amount of risk

No more than 10 per cent of your trading capital should be risked on any single position and no more than 30 per cent on all positions combined. The purpose of such an approach is to limit the adverse effect that a single bad decision can have on an account. It is a strong safeguard against disaster and should be followed scrupulously by anyone who hopes to make profits consistently in futures markets. Unfortunately it will probably be ignored by the very people who would profit by the advice, namely, the inveterate plungers who have visions of making their fortunes in a few months and inevitably end up losing most of their speculative capital on one or two transactions. The importance of limiting risk relative to risk capital available cannot be stressed too strongly. Someone who repeatedly risks a substantial portion of his resources cannot withstand even one loss, and in commodities, as in all other speculative endeavours, losses do occur and must be expected. To pretend otherwise, or to fail to make adequate allowances for adversity, is to ignore reality, which is hardly the key to success anywhere, least of all in futures markets.

Broker's commission and profit objective
Another useful guideline is to pay attention to brokers' commissions in relation to profit objective. Every financial endeavour entails a certain cost, and commissions are the cost of doing business in the futures markets. Their influence on an account can vary widely depending on the average sizes of the profits (and losses) involved. Therefore it becomes imprudent to take a position in the market unless your profit objective is at least eight to ten times your commission cost.

Irrelevance of original margins
One of the characteristics of commodity trading that probably most attracts traders is the leverage afforded by low original margins—sometimes referred to as deposits. Original margins are frequently at the broker's discretion and usually around 10 per cent of the contract value. The volatility of a market will often determine the level of the margin, and margins for high-risk commodities are frequently raised to protect the broker from his client and the client from himself. Seldom do original margins reach the percentage proportion of those required on the Stock Exchange, but of course all original margins must be kept intact and losing market positions require compensating margin amounts to be added to the original outlay.

One of the most common errors that commodity traders make is that of using original margin requirements as a guideline for judging their profits and losses. Some commodity literature advises doing precisely this, which is unfortunate, because it represents a kind of negative contribution to traders' knowledge. As mentioned before, commissions and net trading capital are the appropriate yardsticks with which to measure trading objectives. Original margin is irrelevant to this purpose because it is not a cost, a purchase price, a measure of value or a measure of available capital. In commodity trading, original margin is a security deposit and nothing more.

TRADING EFFECTIVELY

Having spent most of this chapter until now on the aspects of money management and control in relation to commodity investment, we should now turn to the opportunities that the commodity markets offer. There are

a myriad of events which affect the basic Production/Consumption ratio
which in essence decides the course of commodity prices, and therefore
futures prices, from season to season, or even from decade to decade. It is
important therefore that traders should do as much as they can, by
fundamental analysis, to keep abreast of economic and political developments. The financial and national press, economic journals and brokers'
reports can provide much of the news of pertinent material developments
(*see* Chapter 9). It is the Production/Consumption ratio, plus the possibility of a significant carry-over of physical material from one marketing
season to the other, which creates the futures price trend, and one of the
most vital principles of investment is to "trade with the trend". Most
brokers will stress the maxim "never buck the trend" and most brokers
who maintain graphs of price movement are aware of which commodities
have been moving in an up- or down-trend.

When to buy and sell

Seldom can it be said that a commodity is cheap or is dear. It is either
comparatively or historically high-priced or low-priced. An historically
low-priced commodity which is indicating a move into an up-trend is
obviously an attractive potential market for buying. Conversely an
historically high-priced commodity which is developing a down-trend
pattern is an attractive potential for a "short sale". It should be remembered
that in commodities it is just as simple to sell short as to buy long. In fact,
often the rate of decline of market prices can be greater than that of the
incline. Remember the cardinal rules—if in doubt stay out and on no
account trade against the trend.

Liquidating a contract

It is never the intention of the private investor when he buys futures to
take delivery of (*i.e.* receive on his doorstep) 10 tons of cocoa or 50 tons of
sugar, etc.; nor is it his intention to go to the market place in order to
deliver physical goods against his short position. The futures markets
cater for this, allowing for all traders to re-sell or re-buy ("liquidate")
their contracts before maturity date, which, in order to avoid physical
material involvement, they must do. Of course, there are sections of the
industry who from time to time, in order to meet their trade commitments,
will physically deliver or take delivery of the commodity itself when their
contract reaches maturity. This involvement subjects the mature delivery
months to special influences. It is important therefore that the outsider
does not get involved in such circumstances and essential that contracts
are "liquidated" well before the owned delivery month reaches maturity—
in other words do not be involved in delivery months which can act
irrationally owing to maturing physical pressures.

Being selective

Before commencing trading in commodities it is necessary to be selective. It is advisable to avoid becoming involved in thin markets—that is, markets with a consistently low volume of contracts. Nor should there be involvement in an inactive month—some quoted months fail to attract industry interest and have a low liquidity ratio.

Increasing one's position

There are some sensible guidelines when considering increasing one's position. When it is established that a position taken in the market is working out well and the direction of prices is confirming one's judgement, it often appears desirable to add additional contracts to the position. This can be a successful procedure if it is done according to a conservative plan and not merely plunging because of one's enthusiasm. Prudence urges two rules in connection with adding to one's position:

1. Do not add to your position unless your last previously acquired contract shows a profit.
2. Do not add more contracts at any one time than the number of contracts in your original, base commitment.

If the original, base commitment was for more than one or two contracts, then it is advisable that additions should be on a progressively smaller scale. Point 1 above is self-explanatory. The following illustration will make point 2 clear: "X" stands for the number of contracts acquired, reading up from the bottom of the diagrams.

	Desirable	*Not desirable*
Third addition	X	X X X X
Second addition	X X	X X X
First addition	X X X	X X
Initial position	X X X X	X

This procedure is termed "pyramiding". The diagram on the left illustrates pyramiding in a desirable way because it results in an average cost of all contracts at a level conservatively below the market; one's total position is not as vulnerable. The diagram on the right is the result of being carried away with one's enthusiasm (plunging) in a way which results in one's average cost being closer to the market, with the whole position in jeopardy when a moderate reaction occurs.

Spreads or straddles

A good percentage of trading activity in futures markets comprises arbitraging transactions between various delivery months and between markets interrelated but in different world centres. These operations are called "spreads" or "straddles", both meaning the same thing and purely a variation of trade terminology. Spreads or straddles differ from outright sales or purchases in the following manner. An outright sale or purchase represents one transaction at the time of entry into a market and the objective is to realise profits through a rise or fall in prices. A spread or a straddle entails both of these operations at the same time and the objective is to make a profit out of the movement of the spread difference; *e.g.* a trader buys December sugar at £52 per ton and simultaneously sells May sugar at £47 per ton, and by doing this establishes an opening straddle. Subsequently the market price of December sugar moves up to £58 while, owing to some economic reason, the price of May in the same period moves up to £50 only. The straddle (spread) can then be closed (liquidated) by selling December at £58 and simultaneously buying May at £50—a difference of £8 between December and May prices. When this is compared with the opening straddle difference of £5 it can be seen that a gross profit of £3 per ton for each straddle has been secured (December bought at £52, sold at £58 = £6 profit per ton; May sold at £47, bought at £50 = £3 loss per ton).

It is obvious that profit potential from straddle operations is considerably more limited than that for outright transactions, but so, too, is the loss risk considerably reduced. The very fact that straddle business is a prominent component part of trading is confirmation that selectivity of the right month (or market) is extremely important in all transactions. When looking at the foregoing straddle example, how much more profitable it would have been for outright purchases to have been made in the December contract rather than in the May contract.

Because of the necessity for foreign exchange facilities, all commodity business originated in the United Kingdom and directed to overseas futures exchanges must first have Bank of England approval. The Bank of England will only consider firms within the appropriate industry as candidates to qualify for hedging requirements. Thus international arbitrage (spreading), although a factor in commodity prices, is not a section of trading in which the UK private investor may become involved.

Contango, forwardation and backwardation

"Contango", "forwardation" and "backwardation" are market terms used in everyday commodity jargon. A contango market and a forwardation market are exactly the same thing, again a variation of terminology. Such a market is where the near months are priced at a discount to the forward months. A backwardation market is a market where the nearest delivery month commands a premium over the next and ensuing months. Generally speaking, a contango or a forwardation market results from an abundance of an immediately available physical commodity and a back-wardation market indicates a shortage. It is the availability of supply, or the expected availability of supply, in relation to consumption which has a major part in determining the price-related pattern of quoted months in every futures market. Seasonal factors also exert an immensely important influence on short-term price movements (as well as long-term) of many commodities, particularly in the case of foodstuffs.

There is no maximum price difference between months when a market is in backwardation. There is no economic factor (except supply/demand) to restrict the nearer month from assuming any degree of premium over a more forward month. However, a contango market is different. The discount of one month to the next month can be controlled by predetermined costs. The professional financier and those most intimate with the markets are well aware of these costs, which can be defined as: storage costs, insurance costs, finance costs and broker's commission.

To take an example, a financier sees that he can buy January coffee at a price £12 below the price at which he can sell March coffee. He calculates that if he were to go into the market and buy January and take delivery of the physical coffee which he must pay for in full, hold the coffee, pay warehouse storage charges and insurance until March, when he would physically deliver the coffee back to the market, at which time he would receive payment in full, then he would secure a certain rate of interest on his money which was committed for the two months. If this interest is a higher rate per annum than he can secure from other fixed-interest opportunities, then, provided he is sure that the January coffee he purchased is re-deliverable back to the market in March, he may well become involved in containing the straddle difference between January and March.

This example of financing the commodity is termed a "cash and carry" and is particularly prominent in non-perishable commodities such as metals. From the example of cash-and-carry operations it can now be seen that money interest rates have influences on the commodity markets, especially on the straddle differences when nearer positions are at a discount to forwards.

Technical analysis services

What is technical analysis? Technical analysis is the term used for studying and predicting price performance in both the stock markets and commodity markets through the medium of charts. Followers of this system are labelled "chartists". This has nothing to do with fundamental analysis, to which reference has been made earlier (both are dealt with in detail in the following chapter). However, as in the stock market there are a wealth of chartists in the commodity world—they look at charts and nothing else. The extent of their commodity following is such that prices are

affected by their impact, and knowledge of the charting system is well
worth while. Many professional fundamentalists, before making their
hedging decisions, prefer to check on chart considerations. Conversely
there are some chartists who take into account the fundamental situation—
not like the one in the United States who is reported to have his chart
folder rubber-stamped "I am a chartist, do not confuse me with facts"!
In reality the chartist's objective is to decide the future course of prices by
appraising the trends of the past and present, and, although there are many
varying techniques, most systems contain the basic selling or buying
pressure studies. An assessment of what the chartist's position or expected
position is in the markets can be useful in checking accuracy of conclusions
derived from fundamental data. Technical analysis services and teaching
are available in most countries of the western world.

Buying options

This chapter would be far from complete without reference to the very
important subject of commodity options. The past few years and particularly 1973, when nearly all world commodity markets developed major
bull trends, have seen an immense growth in option business.

As we saw in Chapter 3, a commodity option gives the buyer (or
"taker") the right to buy from (or sell to) the seller (or "giver") of the
option at any time within an agreed period, a specified quantity of the
commodity on which the option has been taken, at a price agreed at
the time of the contract; this is known as the basis (or "striking") price.
For this privilege, the taker of the option has to pay a premium to the
giver.

The main attraction of buying an option is that the loss is limited to the
premium. Thus a speculator can take an interest in a market, knowing
what his maximum loss will be; he can also, in commodities, trade under
cover of his option without increasing his liability. He should remember
that he is not buying (or selling) the commodity but simply paying for the
right to buy (or sell) at a price agreed at the time of the contract.

The speculator should be concerned only with buying options. Granting
(selling) of options is for the sophisticated insider; unless the granter is in
the physical end of the commodity (owns physical stocks, processes or has
an extremely intimate involvement) then the potential risk is unacceptable
and should be avoided at all costs.

To take an example of buying an option. A private investor has come to
the conclusion that the zinc market has been in an up-trend for six months
and that everything points to a continuing move upwards. However, the
fact that the market is already looking historically high gives him concern
and he feels that outright purchases are potentially too risky. He finds
from his broker that he can buy the three-months forward option contract

at a premium of £10 per ton when the market (or basis) price is £200 per ton. He decides to buy the option (or two or more, which would give him more flexibility), for which he pays £10 per ton. This £10 per ton is committed and is irretrievable. The zinc market then moves up to £215 per ton. The buyer of the option sells the market at £215. He is then in a position of owning the option, which gives him the right to buy at £200 and is sold on the market at £15 above—a profit of £5 per ton less his commission costs. However, at this stage there is no point in exercising the option. Options should not be exercised until the stated declaration date. The zinc market could well fall back to £200 again, at which point the investor re-buys his short sale at £215, taking a profit of £15 per ton, and maintains his option. If the market fluctuations are frequent enough then the investor has the facility of trading to and fro many times, without increased liability, before finally exercising or even abandoning the option. This is limited liability trading; there is a known cost and the only amount committed is the option premium plus the broker's commissions.

This example typifies a successful operation against a call option. In the case of the put option, the buyer simply is looking for a down-trend. He buys the put option expecting the market to fall—if his judgement is right then he can buy in the market against his option without further liability. The double option offers the buyer both chances but normally costs twice the premium of a single put or call.

There are many traders who see no point in giving up an option premium. They believe options to be an unduly expensive insurance against losses. At times this is difficult to argue with, but when the premiums for a twelve-months option get down to below 10 per cent of the market price (and they have from time to time been considerably lower) then a considered trading programme incorporating the purchasing of options, without doubt, should be a worthwhile study.

Grouping financial resources

Throughout the countries which maintain commodity exchanges there are either brokers or financiers who will offer their services to private investors and in this manner are able to group the smaller investors' resources into one unit with the intention of gaining the advantage of greater financial strength. Commodity futures funds have been founded in non-sterling areas, but their track record has been disappointing. Such a fund in the United Kingdom does not come within the Department of Trade and Industry regulations and to date marketing has been impossible. A commodity futures fund should not be confused with a commodity fund which refers to a unit trust in commodity shares on the Stock Exchange. A number of these funds have been launched successfully.

There is nothing against grouping of financial resources so long as the management of the investment is well informed, owns or has access to in-depth commodity research departments, has easy access to the markets and, of course, measures up to all the respectability and substance necessitated by anyone handling investment for third parties.

Earlier it was asserted that trading in commodities is simplicity itself. Taking profits out of the market is something else and understandably so, when it is recognised that everybody is attempting to achieve the same purpose. Somebody must lose because for every profit in the market there is an equivalent loss. Perhaps some of the foregoing elementary ground-rules will assist readers in finishing on the winning side.

Finally remember: "If in doubt stay out and always trade with the trend."

Chapter 7

Methods of Forecasting Prices

T. H. STEWART

Partner, Investment Research

When you have decided on a broker, the next most important thing is to decide what to buy or sell, unless you give the broker complete discretion.

The common-sense approach is to buy those commodities which are scarce and sell those which are in over-supply, but common sense needs to be used with caution here. Unlike shares, the higher the price of a commodity goes, the more tends to be produced, and, the lower the price goes, the more tends to be used. The opposite to the common-sense approach might therefore prove more profitable in the long run: one well-known trader's motto was "Sell famine, buy glut."

Still dealing in generalities, it is quicker to cope with a famine in wheat (which takes one year to grow) than a shortage of copper, where a new mine will take several years to dig, without mentioning the roads and railways which will be needed to get the stuff away. Therefore it would be likely that trends in the vegetable commodities would be shorter than in the metals—were it not for the fact that consumption of metals is far more variable according to worldwide booms or slumps than consumption of food.

FUNDAMENTAL ANALYSIS

Regression analysis

There are always two sides to the equation in the commodity markets, consumption and production. Both are susceptible to interference from "acts of God" and, even more important, political events or decisions. None the less, the analyst of the commodity markets must take a view of the facts affecting prices such as long-term trends in uses, the possibility of the development of substitutes and the levels of futures trading. The fundamental analyst's most useful tool in attempting to forecast future price levels is probably simple or multiple regression analysis. This, quite simply, is the correlation of two factors, say prices against stocks. On a piece of arithmetic paper, the analyst constructs two axes, the vertical axis representing average annual prices, the horizontal axis representing the level of stocks. Taking a period of twenty-five years, for instance, he can then plot twenty-five points on the chart where average prices and stocks correspond for each year. Simple observation will then enable the analyst to draw a freehand regression line roughly between the thickest concentration of dots. If all the points are on a straight line, the correlation is clearly high: if the dots are random, of course, it would be as well to find other correlations. The object of the exercise is to be able to work out from one factor (stocks, representing supply in this equation), which the analyst hopes to be able to work out accurately, the other factor (price). Where a straight line up from the horizontal axis meets the freehand regression line, that will define the average price level to be expected. Comparing two simple factors as in the above example is simple regression analysis; when you consider three or more it becomes multiple regression analysis.

Figure 7.1 shows a plot of cocoa prices (US cents/lb) against availability, based on estimated stocks at the beginning of the season plus production during the season, for the years 1947 to 1972. A freehand straight line has also been added to the plot. There are more sophisticated ways of estimating the straight line and descriptions can be found in any elementary book on statistics, for example in *Business and Economic Forecasting* by Spencer,

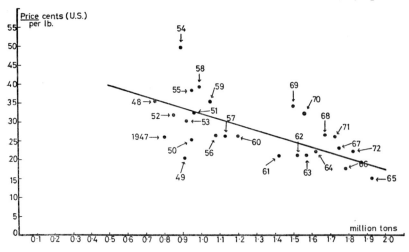

Courtesy: Investment Research

Fig. 7.1. Plot of cocoa prices (US cents/lb) against availability (million tons), 1947–72. The figures are derived from statistics compiled by the Gill & Duffus Group.

Clark and Hoguet, but the eventual line is unlikely to be very different to that plotted "by eye" for most sets of data. There does appear to be a relationship between price level and supply, although an alternative interpretation is that the points cluster randomly about some particular point for the 1950s and about a different point for more recent years.

Naturally enough, stocks and price are not the only factors susceptible to this sort of treatment; you can correlate rates of change in the level of stocks and prices for instance and in this case the axes will cross so that a minus figure can be provided for. In one sense the more long-term the forecast the more difficult it is to make; in another, however, the shorter-term forecasts can be more easily thrown off course by freak weather conditions or something of that sort. The analyst, no matter how sure of his long-term forecasts, can never be quite certain that this year may not deviate from the regression line; also of course an average price can be a mean between very wide swings. The analyst's employer is likely to be at least as interested in a six-month as in a six-year view.

Analysing supply and demand

The trader, whether he is a speculator in futures, or a manufacturer or producer protecting his profit margins, clearly needs to have a view on whether his commodity is fundamentally in over-supply or not. The obvious statistics to watch are those for worldwide production and consumption which can fairly easily be estimated in the case of the non-communist world, but can often only be guessed at in the case of the communist countries, particularly Russia and China. The factors affecting each commodity are different and must be dealt with separately.

Cocoa is used for chocolate all over the world. It is produced only in a few countries, however, notably those of West Africa and Brazil. Weather conditions are clearly important here as local conditions can severely influence the size of the crop. On the other side of the equation, however, chocolate is a luxury and is therefore rather price sensitive: if the price goes up, people eat less of it and manufacturers add more nuts, or milk, to the bar.

Sugar is used all over the world although it is influenced by such factors as a report that saccharine and cyclamates are bad for the health. Demand tends to grow at a steady rate of 3 per cent per annum as the world population increases and becomes richer. Sugar is grown as cane or beet more or less all over the world also, so that localised weather conditions have less effect unless they are particularly severe and reinforce trends already operating owing to government policy. Thus after Castro came to power in Cuba, he contracted to supply a certain tonnage of sugar annually to Russia (to take the place of the contracts previously agreed with the United States by his predecessor). Not only did nationalisation of the sugar plantations lead to a decline in output, but a disastrous hurricane forced the Cuban Government to buy in the open market to make up its commitment to the Russian Government. Here natural trends were reinforced by political decisions and by the fact that only a relatively small proportion of the world's output of sugar is sold on the free market; the rest is protected from outside competition by direct government intervention. Therefore the free market is either the dustbin into which all the world's surplus is dumped or the only source of spare sugar to make up deficits.

The problem with coffee is different. Until recently, only Robusta coffee was dealt with in London (a dollar Arabica contract was started in 1973) and this is about a quarter of the world's output, mostly coming from East Africa and Angola. Brazilian coffee and the Arabicas are not the same thing and the prices of these coffees can move in opposite directions. However, a frost in Brazil, by reducing the surplus, will still tend to affect the London coffee market as few people will notice the difference between different types when they have been made up into Nescafé or Maxwell House. The crucial factors have been the behaviour of the main buyer, the United States, which accounts for about 41 per cent of the total consumption.

Rubber is mainly grown in Malaysia. Because of the time it takes to grow a tree, the supply is relatively inelastic, unless you tap the tree more often, but the demand is not. Here a vital factor is substitution. However, with the price of petroleum now going up, the price of synthetic rubber is also rising. Wars and rumours of wars tend to have an extreme effect on the rubber price because of the slowness of supply to respond to demand and because of sudden purchases by the communist governments.

Wool is mostly grown in Australia. Weather conditions there will affect the price. Recently, a disastrous drought coupled with low wool prices led to a decline in the size of the flock which of course cannot be quickly replaced. When a subsequent flood killed more sheep the following year, this had a dramatic effect on the price which is currently the highest this century. Against this, substitution from synthetic fibres has tended to keep the price down.

Silver is in short supply: consumption exceeds production. However, the market is still overhung by enormous stocks dating from the days when it was used as currency. As silver is mainly produced as a by-product of lead, the two questions are: at what price will the hoarders of silver now be prepared to sell to manufacturers and, in the future, at what price will users decide to do without or to substitute?

Unfortunately the answers to such questions cannot be found by purely rational analysis. In the case of copper, for example, it is easy to say that, because demand is booming and there are difficulties on the supply side, the price is likely to go up. How much is it likely to go up by? If the price is £500 a ton and rising, and the world deficit is estimated at 5 per cent, will a 10 per cent rise in price encourage marginal producers sufficiently and discourage enough marginal consumers to re-establish a new equilibrium? Not necessarily, because you do not know how many speculators will push the price up, some of them being manufacturers building up stocks which they will ultimately use and others building up holdings which they hope ultimately to resell at a profit. Of course, once the price starts coming down, the speculative holder will try to unload and the manufacturer will run his stocks down to a bare minimum, hoping to replenish them at lower prices. Natural instability is thereby reinforced. Therefore, however extravagant a move, either up or down, may seem, do not assume that exceptionally high prices will not be followed by even higher ones. Without throwing common sense out of the window, allow for other people doing so, or being forced to do so. For instance, if a manufacturer thinks the price is high he may sell short: if he is then forced to close, however high the price is in terms of long-term supply and demand, the long term is no longer a factor to be reckoned with until that manufacturer has closed.

TECHNICAL ANALYSIS: CHARTING

Statistics on supply and demand are readily available at reasonable prices—for instance, the World Bureau of Metal Statistics publications. The trouble is that what is known to you is also known to most of the other people who are interested as well, sometimes in greater detail. One of the most popular methods of forecasting prices on the commodity exchanges therefore has been the use of charts, where they are far more widely used than on the Stock Exchange. The argument used by the chartist is: "Follow the other fellow: he probably knows more about the fundamentals than I do." This reduces analysis, of course, to analysis of the price series alone, usually with the assistance of volume and open interest or stock figures. The basic tenet of the chartist, thus jumping on the bandwagon once someone else has started it, is: "A trend continues until it stops."

From this tenet, two problems emerge: (1) how do you recognise a trend, and (2) how do you tell if it has stopped?

Starting from a well-defined base area or reversal pattern, a perfect up-trend proceeds thus: an initial rise is followed by a smaller setback, followed by a new rise to higher prices, followed by a smaller setback (perhaps to the support formed by the immediately previous minor peak), followed by another rise to a new, higher peak, followed by a further smaller setback, and so on *ad infinitum*, in such a manner that the minor setbacks fall on a regular straight line which defines the up-trend, joining two or more of the minor lows, preferably more than two (the more points on a trend line, the more valid it is). A trend is a kind of stable disequilibrium. (The price in a trend obviously is not in equilibrium, or otherwise the price would not be changing, but the disequilibrium has a stability of its own which restricts the movements of the price within the boundaries of the trend channel.) Clearly the price is unlikely to move in the same direction every day—there are always profit takers—which is why you get minor reactions. The three charts we shall use as illustrations all contain trends. Although we have, for purposes of illustration, drawn in some of the trends, they are not difficult for the amateur to recognise.

Much more difficult is to decide whether the up-trend or down-trend (which is exactly the same pattern reversed—read "lower" for "higher", "low" for "peak" and "rally" for "setback") has stopped. It is by no means unusual for a major trend to be interrupted by a substantial pause as a new, temporary, equilibrium is established. This pause is quite likely to break the first, steep up-trend, but until a new confirmed down-trend is established it is rash to assume that the previous trend is reversed, although it would be prudent to adopt a neutral stance until the equilibrium has been upset and a new trend has been confirmed. "Confirmation" consists in a rise to point A, a fall which is smaller than the preceding rise and a new rise to a point above A, which will *ipso facto* give the charts the minimum two points needed for a new trend.

A most interesting example is the chart for New York silver up to the top in May 1968 (*see* Fig. 7.2). Here there is a positive plethora of trends and, because of the fundamental factors affecting the market, the main upward move is interrupted by two significant secondary corrections in January and March. The trend lines join the closing prices, not the extremes, which we believe to be orthodox. Clearly the breaking of a trend line would have been a point to reverse the commitment: in this case the swings were large enough to make this worth while, but a general rule is "always trade with the main trend", as most commodities are one-way markets to a far greater degree than silver. (As we have said before, silver is fundamentally in deficit so far as production is concerned, but the market is overhung by an enormous hoard of bullion, and at some price the hoarders will sell, sometimes for reasons quite other than commodity factors. The Chinese Government unloaded several million ounces in the period under review because they needed the foreign exchange.)

However, the other two examples, copper (London) in 1970 (Fig. 7.3) and cocoa (London) in 1973 (Fig. 7.4) show steady major trends broken

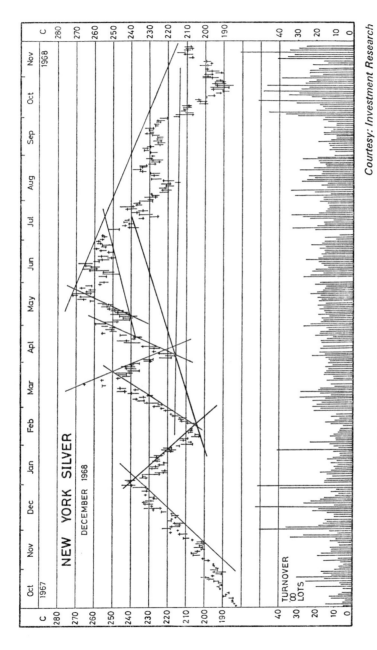

Fig. 7.2.   Bar chart: New York silver (December 1968).

by no significant reactions which would have made trading against the main trend profitable.

Now we must consider reversals. Basically they are of two types— "spearhead" and formal patterns. By "spearhead" we mean a situation where a previous trend, which will probably have been steepening, is abruptly reversed on one day. A minor example will be seen in the middle of March in the silver chart (Fig. 7.2). Typically, this was accompanied by a large "gap" on either side (the day's trading did not overlap at any point with the previous day's trading as enthusiasm turned to hectic speculation and was followed by determined profit-taking turning to panic). The daily permissible limit rules accounted for this, which is why turnover was so low. Spearhead bottoms were seen in spectacular form in coffee and cocoa in 1965, and spearhead tops were seen in cocoa in 1968, in coffee in 1968, in sugar in 1972, and on several other occasions.

Formal patterns tend to occur in equilibrium situations. The most dramatic examples are the "lines" (a long period of trading at almost the same price) in copper in 1962 and 1963 and in silver up to May 1967. In both cases, the major supplier (the big mining groups and the US Treasury respectively) had fixed the price: when the supply ran out, the rise was dramatic. Much more usual are the looser patterns formed by the less formal equilibria arrived at between producers and users. All three charts show some form of this. In the case of New York silver (Fig. 7.2), you can see the building up of a classic "head and shoulders" reversal between April and July 1968.

In three weeks silver had risen from 215 to 260 and then dropped back to 240. This was still a level of very substantial support; over 5000 lots of 10,000 ounces had been traded on the day it was reached, 29 December 1967. The reaction was reversed on this support; and in the next fortnight the position advanced through the level of the spearhead top and was traded for two days above 270. In this fortnight volume never exceeded 2000 lots in a day.

The top was reached on 20 May, a Monday; and on the Tuesday there was a trading range of 10 points and the position closed at the bottom of it. Volume rose over 2000 lots. The subsequent rally was feeble; even when an upward gap appeared on 24 May the volume contracted. A breakaway gap downward then appeared, between the dealings of 27 and 28 May; this was followed by a break for a holiday. The downward movement turned out to be quite short; it terminated at 246 on 4 June. The rally lasted only five trading days; and the subsequent reaction, which lasted as long, traversed an even shorter distance.

At this stage one could see that the whole character of the trading had changed. The old patterns, in which inner trend lines had been extremely useful, had been superseded by a new pattern of shorter and shorter movements. The strong rises and deep reactions before had formed parts of a rising trend. The movements and counter-movements now were quite short. Volume had fallen away a lot from the levels of mid-winter; since the May peak the bigger days had been associated with declines of price rather than rises. There was a change of feeling in the market, and this was expressed in the new pattern that had been developing. Two famous chart formations had appeared at this stage. The tops of April, May and June, with the May top above those of April and June, formed a "head and shoulders" top with an uptilted neckline drawn through the bottoms of early May and early June. The "head" and "right shoulder" formed a triangle. When New York opened after the holiday of 4 July, silver broke downwards out of these patterns in a sharp two-day decline with volumes over 2000 and 3000 lots. That looked like, and for a long time at any rate was, the end of the bull market in silver.

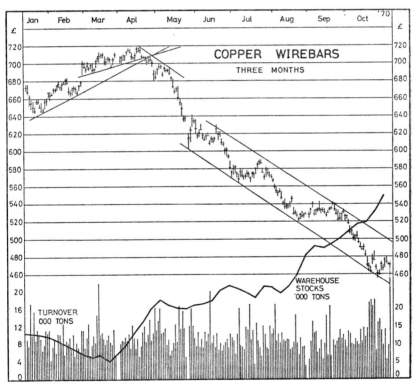

Fig. 7.3.   Bar chart: London copper (1970).

At the beginning of 1970, copper wirebars ran up to £702 at the start of March and then traded gently upwards to a peak, reached on three consecutive days, at £718 in the second week of April (*see* Fig. 7.3). During these six and a half weeks there was a well-defined lower trend line, but a very gentle one in comparison with what had gone before in the earlier part of 1969 when copper rose from £450 to reach £710 in December. It was clear that the metal was passing through a period of informal equilibrium from that December peak onwards. The decline about the New Year had proved abortive, and now, in the spring, wirebars were trading in a narrow range, slightly uptilted, which could have proved the springboard for a new, dramatic rise. It is worth pointing out that a very large backwardation, of up to £100, existed at the time. The old adage "Where there's a back there's a drop" should not be taken more seriously as a means of forecasting the future than adages about St Swithin's Day or red skies and the delight or otherwise of shepherds in forecasting the weather: both are not wholly without foundation but should not be relied upon heavily.

In the third week of April, the price fell out of the minor up-trend by a small margin. More significantly, the more important up-trend joining the lows of end January and end February was also broken, but again by a small margin only. However, the down-trend was confirmed by a downward break leaving a large gap on 27 April: the subsequent rally was turned back by the underside of the seven-week trading area which preceded it and on 12 May the price broke below £680 for the first time since February. Here then you have a steep secondary down-trend joining the peaks of 15 April and 10 May (in this case we have not joined the daily closing price but the extremes for the sake of clarity: the effect is the same in either case) with peaks below peaks and lows below their predecessors. In due course a well-defined trend was established with slightly diverging upper and lower trend lines, and this was maintained for the rest of 1970.

Our final example is cocoa, the May 1973 contract (*see* Fig. 7.4). Here again, there was a good bull market in the commodity starting in February 1972 which took the commodity up (in this contract) from below £230 to £320 in the first week of September. The final, steep phase is shown. The upward trend was broken on 19 September, but the price was soon equalled although not exceeded on a closing-price basis. Throughout October and November another informal equilibrium was established between £310 and £325. It would have been as well to have been out of the market at this period or for the manufacturer to have kept his books straight. On 12 December the price broke out of the trading range upwards on good volume, with a gap again.

Unfortunately the price then fell back into the trading range again and compounded the discomfiture of the bulls by proceeding to fall out of the October–November range downwards, also on good volume, on 19 January. All of this, incidentally, was within the 10 per cent margin range of a bull who had taken up a position at, say, £326 or £329. Although the late September low at £300 remained inviolate, it would have been a very determined speculator indeed who did not at that point reverse his position, with a stop-loss presumably at £330, or at least close out his position. The subsequent history can be seen. The demoralised bull would probably not have gone back in below £340, but what a rich harvest he would subsequently have gathered!

Bar charts, which we have discussed so far, are not the only technical method of looking at the market. As widely used are point and figure

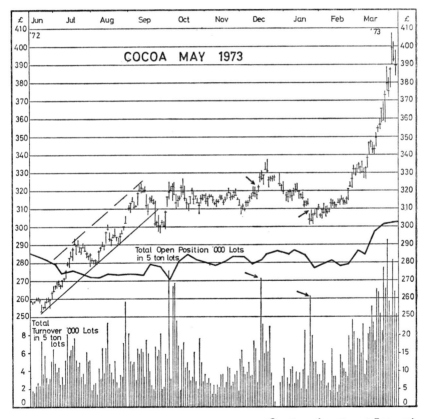

Courtesy: Investment Research

Fig. 7.4.   Bar chart: London cocoa (May 1973).

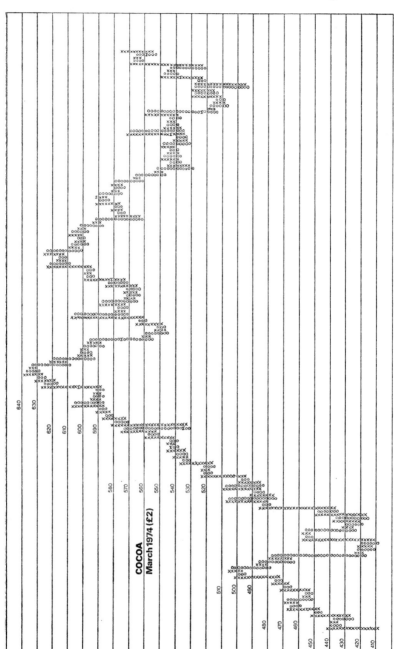

Courtesy: Chart Analysis Ltd

Fig. 7.5.   Point and figure chart: London cocoa (March 1974).

charts which to the uninitiated look like noughts and crosses. A bar chart
has one bar per day: a point and figure chart measures only movement,
"X" upwards and "0" downwards. Thus, there may be no plot one day
and ten the next. As soon as an upward move is completed by a row of
crosses, you move to the next column when the price goes down, marking
a row of noughts. The example illustrated in Fig. 7.5 (for which we are
indebted to Chart Analysis Ltd) is a three-point reversal: *i.e.* the price
must reverse by three units before you move to the next column. This is
the March 1974 cocoa contract, and you will not find less than three
crosses or noughts in any column. The start of a new month is marked by a
number ("1" for January, "2" for February, etc.), and the start of a new
week by "M" for Monday so that you get some idea of chronology.

Apart from enabling you to draw trends and spot the typical reversal
patterns which we have discussed above, the big advantage of the point
and figure method is that you can measure the likely extent of a move.
Thus, if you have a trading block, as in the period marked, you can count
the number of figures horizontally across the thickest part—19—and say
that the price will move up or down out of that area by 19 × 3 × the unit
of measurement (£2 in this case), giving an answer of £114. (You multiply
19 by 3 because this is a three-point reversal chart; if it were a five-point
reversal you would multiply by 5, if a simple one-point reversal you would
only multiply by 1, *i.e.* not at all.) As the final move was down from £540,
you would have a "target" of £426 to aim at. You must, of course, exercise
common sense; a fall below zero is impossible.

Another advantage is that support and resistance levels can appear
much more clearly. What is merely a point on a one-day-per-square bar
chart may be a tight trading block in the point and figure system. Most
commodity brokers who use charts keep up some of both bar and point
and figure. It is more difficult to correlate point and figure charts with
daily volume figures. Also gaps do not appear. On the other hand, you
can use several different scales which will give different pictures in point
and figure but not on bar charts. A £1 scale shows intra-day trading
opportunities: a £10 scale will give in condensed form the whole picture,
which is likely to be helpful in spotting the main trend. It would be sensible
therefore to keep two or three point and figure charts on any one commodity, but only one bar chart would be required.

EVALUATION OF FUNDAMENTAL AND TECHNICAL ANALYSIS

The weakness of fundamental analysis is that you can never be sure if
the facts known to you are all the relevant facts. The best analyses can be

Trading in commodities

overthrown by changes in government policy or essentially speculative decisions on the part of other investors or manufacturers. In the example shown in Fig. 7.4, everything conspired together to help the bull and make the shortage of cocoa yet more chronic: the devaluation of sterling and the dollar, making commodities a currency hedge; the fact that one manufacturer at least sized up the market wrongly; the holding back of supplies by the Ghana Marketing Board, who also paid low prices to the farmers so that supply did not increase as expected while demand remained surprisingly high; and finally unfavourable weather conditions.

The weakness of charts, however, is that false signals are not uncommon: Fig. 7.4 shows two. Of course, a stop-loss policy would have helped the private speculator. If you lose 10 per cent on unsuccessful deals, gain 50 per cent on the successful ones and make one correct decision out of three, you will do well.

The ideal compromise seems to be to use both technical and fundamental analysis: when they agree, the combination seems likely to prove highly profitable. When they disagree in their conclusions, clearly the market should be approached with caution. Experience shows that a fundamental analysis based on regression analysis can forecast long-term trends of price for, in particular, the major metals or sugar, which are less influenced by localised weather conditions and where supply and demand can be forecast with reasonable accuracy some way ahead according to economic models of boom or slump and population growth. Prices will tend to fluctuate around these trends, but it would be wrong to suggest that the amplitude of the fluctuations can be forecast as from time to time special factors will continue to obtrude, and speculators, private and professional, will from time to time take control of markets. If one has confidence in the fundamental analysis, the professional can take advantage of the cyclical swings around the trend to buy or sell more advantageously, but he must guard against the possibility that the cycle may turn into a supercycle, as in 1973. This is where technical analysis should be a useful tool.

Chapter 8

Topics of Relevance to a Businessman

L. A. BRIGHTON
Director, Merrill Lynch, Pierce, Fenner & Smith
(Brokers & Dealers) Ltd

HEDGING AGAINST PRICE RISKS

One of the basic functions of a commodity futures market is to provide facilities where representatives of the commodity trades can hedge their price risks. Simply stated, hedging against price risks is accomplished when a position in the futures market is established approximately equal and opposite to the position held by the hedger in the physical (also known as the actual or cash) market. By doing this, those who handle commodities in their business (growers, distributors, processors, etc.) can protect themselves against loss due to adverse price fluctuations. The hedge taken may involve a short futures position against forward sales of physical commodities not yet in hand. Perhaps a single illustration of one type of hedge will help at this point.

Consider, for example, the price-risk problems of the cotton merchant who has just bought, say, 300 bales of cotton from a grower. The minute he takes title to the physical commodity the risks of all price fluctuations until the cotton is sold become his.

Presumably the price paid to the grower was related to the prevailing price of, say, December cotton futures. To protect himself, therefore, until the cotton is sold to a user or export buyer, the merchant sells three contracts of December cotton futures (300 bales) short on, say, the New York Cotton Exchange. In doing so, the merchant has placed himself in the position of being able to price his product competitively in the market place at all times. If prices should decline, the loss on the value of the physical cotton is offset largely by the profit realised from the short position in December futures. By the same token, if prices should advance, the loss which the merchant would have to take when buying back his short December futures position is expected to be offset by the greater profit he would realise from the sale of his actual inventory. Thus the merchant has freed himself from the worry and risk of price fluctuations

91

so that he can concentrate on his major function in the market place—namely that of accumulating and distributing an inventory of cotton for eventual use by consumers. This would not be possible if there was not always a ready facility for trading in futures offered by the various commodity exchanges.

It can readily be seen that the purpose of the futures markets is to free traders from the rather restricted forms of protection which are all that are available in the physical markets. It also reduces the element of financial risk inherent in holding large quantities of expensive goods surplus to immediate requirements or in lacking such goods should the need for them arise unexpectedly.

The process of hedging, of course, may be flexible. The ideal hedge is always considered that which is applied at the same time that a physical contract is made. However, in practice flexibility is used and on many occasions a hedge can be enhanced by trading on the futures market either just before or just after the physical trade takes place. A manufacturer, for instance, may well have a "continual" or "running" hedge which gives him stability in his buying of physical raw materials and his eventual marketing of the finished articles.

This process of price insurance renders a service of great value by increasing the willingness of banks to lend against commodities. Hedges can protect a bank from serious loss, while unhedged commodities do not provide the same satisfactory security. When advances are made against unhedged commodities, a wide margin is required, and it therefore follows that the system of hedges enables a trader to work with less capital, or, in other words, he can conduct a larger volume of business on his available capital.

Not only do the representatives of the various commodity trades use the futures markets for hedging purposes, but a significantly large number of speculators are attracted to futures trading by the high leverage afforded in the use of one's finances, and by the opportunity for profit which volatile and quickly changing prices produce.

Organised futures exchanges act as a focal point for the dissemination of statistics, weather reports and other information vital to the industries they serve so that we now come to the point where, knowing how hedging works, we can look to how best we can obtain information about our commodity and where to obtain advice about price predictions and the timing of purchases.

PRICE PREDICTIONS AND TIMING OF PURCHASES

Although futures prices in many commodities frequently change rapidly, the interplay of buyers and sellers on a worldwide scale trading in an open competitive market quickly establishes what a commodity is "worth" at any given moment. Since prices are quickly disseminated by tickers and quotation boards, the smallest user of the market has as much knowledge of the prevailing value of the commodity he wishes to buy or sell as the largest user. This is important since, in a free economy, price is the catalyst which facilitates the allocation of goods among potential users, and distributes output most efficiently.

Commodity prices change in response to anticipated or actual shifts in supply–demand relationships—not only for the commodity itself, but for substitute or competing commodities as well. In addition, commodity prices may be affected by changes in farm legislation (by the US Government, through EEC Farm Programmes, etc.), currency rates, the operation of international commodity agreements, and the general commodity price level. Political manoeuvrings also have their bearing on commodity price structures.

The problem of the commodity businessman is to ascertain, to sift and to evaluate those factors which are likely to exert the most influence on the price of a commodity. In order to do this he must first familiarise himself with the basic market structure of the commodity under consideration. For example, if it is an agricultural commodity (a field crop which is planted each year) he should learn when it is planted in major producing areas of the world, what are the major threats to crop development and when it is usually harvested in volume. This knowledge will provide some idea as to the time of year when weather developments are of major importance as a market factor, and when seasonal price pressure from the harvest may usually be expected. Continuing beyond the harvest, he should learn, to the extent that such information is available, the normal marketing pattern and channels of the commodity. This information should provide an idea as to when producers usually market their production and through what channels. Most commodity brokers are in a position to give much information about all commodities, particularly those commodities that have a reasonably strong futures market. Many such brokers publish weekly reviews about various commodities—some even publishing what is known as a daily letter—and, of course, all this information is readily available to the trade free of cost. The information that brokers give in these reports is collected from all possible sources—*e.g.* Reuters Commodity News Service—and through close collaboration from, and a free exchange of information with, producers and other traders in the same commodity. There are brokers who specialise in various commodities, but in recent years there has been a distinct move to diversify so that as a result practically all leading brokers are departmentalised with experts in each commodity and even large departments handling just one very active and international commodity. Such brokers that handle a significant amount of commodity futures business have available a commodity research department whose function is to maintain records of statistical information and to provide interested clients with this information usually with their interpretation of its significance to price action and suggestions as to possible trading opportunities.

The final responsibility and decision to enter into a transaction usually rests with the individual trader, but the client may ask his broker to obtain pertinent information relating to a specific commodity or market situation. The trader may take it from there, studying the information available and forming his own opinion of the profit and risk possibilities before entering a trade.

The timing of purchases is of course dependent on so many factors—the current price structure of a commodity, what is already "written in" to the price for forward delivery, whether supplies will be readily available (even at a price), how much inventory should be carried, bank rate, cost of carrying raw materials, general overheads and, finally, whether the price of the finished article will make it reasonably saleable. It is not always easy to find a solution to these problems, especially in periods of world-wide economic uncertainty. But the futures market does help to iron out much of the price-risk factor and goes a long way to relieving some of the worry and anxiety confronting the businessman.

Probably the most logical way to proceed with the evaluation of the price prospects for a particular commodity is to start with an analysis of those factors which constitute the supply. As a generalisation, changes in supply resulting from shifts in the production outlook within a season, being of a more dramatic nature, tend to receive more market attention than changes in demand. Supply consists of inventory (carry-over) at the start of the marketing year, plus the season's production and estimated imports (if of any consequence). The carry-over can be broken down into the portion which is in commercial hands ("free" stocks) and that which is still in producers' hands and still unsold. Having determined the factors making up supply, comparing the figures with those for previous years and evaluating their probable importance as a price-making influence, the market analyst must relate indicated supply prospects to anticipated demand.

The demand, itself, of course, can be affected by the price structure of a commodity; *i.e.* too high a price for too long a period will slow the demand. Other factors, domestically, would have a bearing on demand such as high interest rates, general inflation and other seasonal factors. For most commodities in the United Kingdom, the Department of Trade and Industry is a very good source of information although there is a time factor in all statistics issued by it. While most businessmen would know quite a lot about the commodities they handle daily, there is not always the free flow of information within those commodities and so it would always be helpful to subscribe to statistical information such as that just mentioned or approach a broker who concentrates on those commodities of special interest. The whole purpose of analysing supply and demand statistics is to enable the students of the market, whether they be members of the trade or traders, to arrive at a decision as to the probable future course of prices.

LEVELS OF TRADING

Some traders over the years have been very active, and, in some cases, had it not been for such activity in the futures markets, many a company would not have been able to expand in the way that they have done. There are arguments for and against when it comes to discussing whether one should trade heavily or not. So far as hedging is concerned, then the level of trading in the futures market should reflect the amount of trading in the physical commodity—anything above that performance is speculation. Now, of course, it could be argued that all trading is speculation—perhaps this is so—but it should be remembered that many large trade houses are in possession of an enormous amount of information about the raw materials they use in production, and sometimes a calculated risk can be taken: provided the traders are agile in their trading many a profit and loss account can be improved on. Over-trading, however, can be dangerous, and therefore one should be inclined to keep any trading over and above hedging within the normal bounds of business activity. Over-activity is prone to give the price structure a false look and this, in itself, is wrong.

It is the practice in soft commodities for manufacturers to hold varying degrees of cover depending on the anticipated forward delivery availabilities and price. In general, however, over many years the average cover would be seven or eight months. The writer remembers, not so many years ago, chocolate manufacturers holding cover of over one year. This was exceptional but at the prices obtainable for raw cocoa beans at that time this was the only logical thing to do. In periods of tight supply since then, however, some small chocolate manufacturers have bought only on a hand-to-mouth basis, and for a short time it has been better to do this than hold a large forward position at very high prices.

Generally, when a buyer is at risk on price he should hedge almost at the same time. With good advice from his broker he may be able to trade at a slightly different time in order to take advantage of an already moving market or an anticipated moving market: in any case any hedging activity should not be too far away from the physical purchase—or sale—as this constitutes out-and-out speculation. Information on expected important moves can be readily obtained from a first-class broker. Use prudence at all times. Build a forward position of larger availability when the market warrants it but keep "near at home" when the price structure is high.

Chapter 9

Keeping in Touch
C. W. J. GRANGER

INFORMATION AND THE INVESTOR

Good investment is achieved by combining a sound strategy with accurate and up-to-date information. Four types of information can be distinguished: that relating to the position of current and recent prices and other market movements; information on fundamental qualities such as levels of production or the state of the economy of some important country: the opinions or forecasts of "experts"; and, lastly, research on possible strategies. The first three types are of direct importance when making immediate investment decisions and the last is relevant when deciding on one's philosophy and approach to investing in commodities or in any other risky asset.

The quality and quantity of information one needs depends on how seriously one takes the investment problem. It can vary from taking a casual glance at prices in a newspaper every few days to attempting to keep in touch with all conceivably relevant events at all moments of time. The choice of the amount of time and money spent on information gathering must be left to the individual investor. As a general rule, if one takes a long horizon a more casual approach can be afforded than if one attempts to take a continuing sequence of short-run horizons.

THE STATE OF THE MARKET

For the majority of investors the most vital pieces of information are the market closing prices. Most quality newspapers will provide some kind of price data, so that one can see how one's investment is progressing each morning, although this is not recommended as regular breakfast-time reading except for those with very strong nerves. Commodity prices can fluctuate wildly and a dramatic fall could ruin one's day even though, in the long run, such a single-day fluctuation may be of little consequence.

The papers typically report closing spot and future prices for London and US commodity markets and perhaps also give a brief statement about the direction of the market, although these comments are often imprecisely phrased, using terms such as "irregularly dearer" and "fully firm". One soon gets used to these.

The amount of market information varies considerably, with the *Daily Telegraph* providing some 15 column inches and *The Times* 22 column inches. By far the most detailed reports and clearest tables are provided by the *Financial Times*, which also publishes a weekly review, with some charts, every Saturday. A warning is in order on the US prices quoted. Owing to the difference in time zones the day's closing prices are not available when the first editions are prepared, so that readers of the *Financial Times* in outlying areas of the United Kingdom read Monday night's prices in Wednesday's paper.

Almost unique to the *Financial Times* is the provision of commodity market price indices. These are averages of the prices of a wide range of major commodities, usually with some particularly important commodities being given greater weight than others. Such an index is useful in getting an overall picture of the movements of commodity prices, although it has yet to be proved that these indices are as useful as those provided for the major stock exchanges. Four spot-price indices are provided, the *Financial Times* (based on 11 commodities from both London and US markets), the Dow-Jones (based on 12 commodities, with very large weightings given to wheat and cotton), Moodies (based on 15 commodities) and Reuters (based on 17 commodities, as follows, with weights in parentheses: wheat (14), cotton (13), coffee (11), wool (11), copper (9), sugar (7), rubber (7), maize (5), rice (4), beef (4), soyabeans (3), cocoa (3), tin (2), groundnuts (2), cocoa (2), zinc (2) and lead (1)). From its construction, the Reuters index appears likely to be able to pick up any tendency affecting most commodities and therefore to be most useful. A Dow-Jones futures index is also provided.

Although the most recent prices are obviously of considerable interest, when making a decision about changing an investment, many investors would also like to compare them with previous price changes. A partial solution is given by the *Financial Times*, which also provides prices for a month earlier. However, much more useful data might be derived from charts of prices, in the form either of the plot of prices, both spot and future, through time or alternatively of point and figure charts, examples and explanations of which can be found in Chapter 7. An investor could construct such charts himself, but would find the effort required not inconsiderable. It may be possible to obtain charts from one's broker but one can also purchase excellently produced charts from firms specialising in their production, such as Investment Research (28 Panton Street,

Cambridge CB2 1DH) or Chart Analysis (194–200 Bishopsgate, London EC2M 4PE). Interpretation of the charts is also provided.

For anyone wishing to keep in continuous touch with movements in the market, two services are provided by Reuters Economic Services (85 Fleet Street, London EC4). The printer service (ticker-tape) provides a complete price and news service relating to sugar, grains and oilseeds, metals, cocoa, coffee, wool, rubber and shipping. One can choose to have news about any single commodity or any combination of commodities. A subscription to the Full Commodity Service will provide one with many yards of paper output a day but its format makes it easy to skim through and select the items of particular interest to oneself.

The alternative services provided by Reuters, known as Videomaster and Stockmaster, enable one to request information from a central computer about price, volume and so forth for a very wide range of both commodities and stocks from various exchanges. One simply pushes the necessary keys on the keyboard and the required information is displayed electronically. The Stockmaster displays just a single number at each occasion whereas the Videomaster displays a screen full of numbers instantaneously and also enables one to keep a continuous watch on the prices of up to eighteen stocks or commodities. Such space-age equipment is likely to be merely of academic interest to most investors, but is obviously of great importance to large traders, manufacturers and banks.

It is interesting to compare this Reuters service with the very first service provided in 1850 by the firm, a financial information transmission— by carrier pigeon—between Aachen and Brussels. Apparently pigeons could travel these 100 miles several hours quicker than the available trains and thus filled a gap in the telegraphic service between the two important financial centres of Berlin and Paris. From little acorns . . ..

FUNDAMENTAL INFORMATION, OPINIONS AND FORECASTS

It is important that an investor in commodities should keep in touch with the fundamental data relating to his investment. This will include news on crops or production, levels of government intervention, levels of inventory held by producers, manufacturers or other investors, and statistics relating to economies and interest rates. The news items carried by the ordinary newspapers will not be sufficient for most serious investors and they will need to turn to the financial press, the commodity brokers or specialist firms such as Moodies or Reuters.

By far the most convenient form of this information is the daily, weekly or monthly news-sheets provided by many brokers or the service firms. For example, Reuters will supply daily news-sheets for thirteen commodities or commodity groups, including sugar, metals, cocoa, coffee, wool and rubber. A weekly commodity report covering all markets is provided by Chart Analysis Ltd, and Moodies (6 Bonhill Street, London EC2A 4BU) provide a composite service covering economies, industries and commodities with a monthly *General Survey and Statistical Bulletin* and a quarterly *Basic Review*. The costs of subscription vary considerably, from under £20 to over £100, but trial subscriptions can be obtained from most services. You just "pays yer money and takes yer choice".

The main firms of commodity brokers will also supply irregularly timed reports on each of the commodity markets, both reviewing the recent past and attempting to predict the future. The financial press also provide forward-looking articles about the markets, such as the December Commodity Review in the *Investors Chronicle*. One of the uses of these articles is to point out implications of recent news events that may have escaped the average investor. For very specialised markets one has to approach the firms that concentrate on them: for example, if one is interested in investing in diamonds, one could contact Diamond Selection Ltd (46 Hatton Garden, London EC1), who supply convincing material about the advantages of such an investment.

It is not possible to provide a complete list of the various commodity brokers and service firms, but these firms are allowed to advertise so that a glance at the advertisements in the *Investors Chronicle*, for example, will soon bring many of them to one's attention. When preparing this chapter the companies that supplied useful material, apart from those already mentioned in the text, were Commodity Analysis Ltd (194–200 Bishopsgate, London EC2M 4PE), Wallace Brothers Commodities Ltd (108 Fenchurch Street, London EC3M 5HP), Jeremy Oates Ltd (16 Monument Street, London EC3 R8AJ) and Commodity Management Services Ltd (46 Hay's Mews, London W1X 8LR).

Forecasts of the British and other economies can also be obtained. For example, the National Institute for Economic Research issues quarterly forecasts which are widely reported in the press, and every four months the *Sunday Times* publishes forecasts derived from the large-scale econo-metric model constructed at the London Business School. Although these forecasts will often provide useful insights into what may happen, it must always be remembered that economic forecasting is a well-developed art but still a developing science.

GETTING THE STRATEGY RIGHT

There must be almost as many approaches to investing as there are inves-tors. The fact that very few leave the race either from going bankrupt or from becoming so rich that further wealth is of no consequence suggests that a Darwinian evolutionary theory does not apply sufficiently strongly for bad strategies to be overwhelmed by good ones. It will be the hope of most investors just to do rather better than the average investor. Very few strategies are even put through a proper scientific test and even when this is tried it is found very difficult to devise a sound test or to analyse the results from it.

There is some interest among the academic communities in both the United Kingdom and the United States in investigating commodity markets and some of the work produced is of real importance to an investor, although most is not. There are various, almost insuperable, problems for investors in appreciating this research. It is published in academic journals that are not readily available apart from in university libraries and the papers involve sophisticated use of mathematics, statistics, economics and accounting that are beyond the comprehension of the vast majority of investors and financial analysts. Some books do appear which review this literature, and these are mentioned in the bibliography at the end of the chapter. The other source of knowledge is, or should be, one's broker. The better brokers employ analysts able to appreciate this academic literature or have academic consultants to review it for them. Some brokers even sponsor basic research. It may be worth enquiring about the availability of such a service when choosing one's broker.

However, one must not expect this work to indicate some foolproof strategy. If such a strategy were found, it would hardly be made public, even by an academic. Where the work can help is in deciding how much weight to place on certain types of information, such as the past pattern of prices, and how best to select a portfolio of assets, including commodities, to give one the best expected level of return with the amount of risk one is willing to accept.

There are also available short conferences and courses which could be of help in getting one's philosophy right. These are advertised in the press and should also be known to one's broker. A college specialising in these courses is the New School of Finance (194–200 Bishopsgate, London EC2M 4PE).

BIBLIOGRAPHY

Gerald Gold, *Modern Commodity Futures Trading*, Commodity Research Bureau Ltd, 1968. A well-written, general introduction to futures trading, particularly on the US markets.

G. L. Rees, *Britain's Commodity Markets*, Elek Books, 1972. Particularly strong on the historical and institutional aspects of the markets.

Trading in commodities

Walter C. Labys and Clive W. J. Granger, *Speculation, Hedging and Commodity Price Forecasts*, Lexington Books, 1971. Uses sophisticated statistical analysis to see if one can forecast spot prices using various data including futures prices, supply and demand. Contains a very comprehensive bibliography of academic research up to 1971.

John R. Dominguez, *Devaluation and Futures Markets*, Lexington Books, 1972. Investigates what happened to futures markets around a period when the pound devalued.

Walter C. Labys, *Dynamic Commodity Models*, Lexington Books, 1973. Discusses the uses of econometric models for commodities.

Appendix 1
Glossary

Actuals: The physical commodities—also referred to as "physicals".

Arbitrage: The usually spontaneous purchase of futures in one market against the sale of futures in a different market to profit from a difference in price.

Backwardation: Price differential between nearby and forward quotations when near dates are at a premium.

Basis price: The price agreed between seller and buyer of an option to become the price at which the option can be exercised. The basis price is usually the current market price of the commodity, for the delivery month, at the time the option is sold. (Also "Striking price".)

Bear: One who believes prices will move lower.

Bid: An offer to purchase at a specified price.

Broker: One who executes the buy and sell orders of a customer for a commission.

Bull: One who expects prices to rise.

Call: A period in which trading is conducted to establish the price for each futures month at a particular time.

Call option: A call option gives to the purchaser the right to *buy* a futures contract from the *seller* on the terminal market at an agreed price (the basis price) at any time from time of purchase to the expiry of the option. A call option is bought, therefore, in the expectation of a rise in price.

Clearing house: The separate agency associated with a futures exchange through which futures contracts are offset or fulfilled and through which financial settlement is made.

Comex: The New York Commodity Exchanges—but more commonly used as a market abbreviation for the Copper Price in New York.

Contango: Price differential between nearby and forward quotation when near dates are lower than forward quotation. (Also "Forwardation".)

Day order: Orders that are placed for execution, if possible, during only one trading session. If the order cannot be executed that day, it is automatically cancelled.

Declaration (of options): To exercise his rights under his option the purchaser must make his declaration (through his broker to the broker of the party granting the option) at an agreed, specified time before the prompt date. Failure to do so is construed as abandoning the option.

Delivery month: The month in which the futures contract matures and within which delivery of the physical commodity can be made.

Deposit: The initial outlay required by a broker of a client to open a futures position, returnable upon closure of the position.

Discretionary account: An account for which buying and selling orders can be placed by a broker or other persons, without the prior consent of the account owner for each such individual order.

Double option: A double option provides the purchaser the right to *buy from or sell to* the seller on the futures market a futures contract at an agreed price (the basis price) at any time during the life of the option.
    Essentially, therefore, it is a combined put and call, except that only the put side or the call side of the option may be exercised, not both. None the less, when the purchaser buys more than one option, he may exercise each one independently of the others. A double costs approximately twice a put or call and is used when the purchaser expects the price to move radically, but is not sure which way.

First notice day: The first day on which notices of intentions to deliver actual commodities against futures market positions can be made or received. First notice day will vary with each commodity and exchange.

Floor broker: A representative of a member firm of the commodity market or ring who is "on the floor" (*i.e.* in the market, ready to do business) at all times the market is open. Only floor brokers are permitted to deal in the market and the usual mode of dealing is by "open outcry".

Forwardation: *See* "Contango".

Futures: Contracts for the purchase and sale of commodities for delivery some time in the future on an organised exchange and subject to all terms and conditions included in the rules of that exchange.

Good-til-cancelled (GTC): An order which will remain open for execution at any time in the future until the customer decides to cancel it.

Hedge: The establishment of an opposite position in the futures market from that held in the physicals.

Kerb: Literally means trading conducted outside the exchange on the kerb of the street—nowadays also means on the telephone or any other dealings outside the ring.

Last trading day: The day on which trading ceases for a particular delivery month. All contracts that have not been offset by the end of trading on that day must thereafter be settled by delivery of the actual physical commodity.

Limit: The maximum fluctuation the price may make of a particular commodity during a particular time—usually a day (not applicable to the LME). Appendix 2 cites the various London limits.

Limit order: An order for a futures contract to buy at no more or sell at no less than a specified price. (*See* also "Market order".)

Liquidation: The closing out of a long position. It is also sometimes used to denote closing out a short position, but this is more often referred to as covering.

Long: Starting a transaction by the purchase of a futures contract.

Lot: The minimum unit of contract for a particular commodity. The lot sizes are cited in Appendix 2.

Margin call: A request for funds by a broker to keep the original deposit intact at 10 per cent of the contract value.

Market order: An order to buy or sell a futures contract at whatever price obtainable at the time entered in the market.

Notice day: A trading day during which notices of intention to deliver actual commodities against short positions in the spot month are made.

Open outcry: The usual method of dealing employed in London futures markets (except the rubber market). The broker says, for all to hear, "Buy (or sell) X amount of commodity/delivery at X price". When another broker responds, to take the offer, the deal is thereby fixed and that price becomes the latest traded price for that delivery date of the commodity.

Option: An option provides the investor the right to buy from or sell to the grantor of the option at any time before its expiration a specified quantity of the commodity concerned at an agreed price (the basis price). The cost to the purchaser of the option is called the "premium" and, depending on the volatility of price movements and duration of option, is usually about 10 per cent of the cost of the commodities contract.

Pre-market: Trading among brokers' offices before the rings open. (*See* also "Kerb".)

Premium (options): The price, in effect, paid by the purchaser of the option to the grantor (seller). It is quoted in pounds or pence per unit of measurement (*e.g.* for cocoa: pounds per ton, so that the cost of an option for one 10-ton contract is 10 times the quoted premium; for silver: pence per ounce, so that the cost of an option for one warrant of silver is 10,000 times the quoted premium).

Put option: A put option provides the purchaser the right to *sell* to the grantor of the option on the futures market a futures contract at an agreed price (the basis price) at any time during the life of the option.
   A put option therefore is bought in the expectation of a fall in price.

Ring: The official trading on the London Metal Exchange (*see* pp. 111–12 for ring trading times).

Short: Starting a transaction by the sale of a futures contract.

Spot month: The first deliverable month for which a quotation is available on the futures market.

Squeeze: Pressure on a particular delivery, pushing its price up against the rest of the market.

Stop-loss order: An order which becomes a market order to *buy* only if the market advances to a specified level, or to *sell* if the market declines to a specified level. It is generally used to limit losses but can also be used to initiate new positions. (Also a "Stop".)

Straddle: The usually simultaneous purchase of one futures month and the sale of another either in the same or different commodity, or exchange.

Striking price: *See* "Basis price".

Switching: Transferring an open position into a different delivery of the same commodity (*e.g.* selling three lots of July cocoa and at the same time buying three lots of September cocoa).

Tender: Delivery against a futures contract.

Warrant of settlement: This is documentary evidence of title to a cited quantity of a physical commodity of a certain type and quality, signed by the warehouse in which it is stored. In effect, it is a "demand note" to the warehouse. (The holder of the warrant is responsible for storage and insurance costs of the commodity in question.)

Appendix 2
Basic Trading Information

1. The London Cocoa Terminal Market Association
Lot size. 10 metric tons
Deposit per lot. £150.
Quotations. Pounds sterling and decimals per metric ton.
Minimum fluctuation. £0·50 per metric ton (£5·00 per lot).
Maximum fluctuation. When, during trading hours, there is in respect of any position other than the spot month an accepted bid or trade at £20 below or above the closing price of the previous day, the market will close for 30 minutes and will be reopened with a special call with limitless trading until the close of the day.
Trading positions. Up to 15 months ahead in: March, May, July, September, December.
Brokerage. Non-members, round-turn inclusive of fees £24. Market movement necessary to break even after commission £2·50.
Trading hours. Monday to Friday 1000 hours to 1300 hours, 1430 hours to close of 1650 hours call.
Calls at 1000 hours, 1250 hours, 1530 hours, 1650 hours.

2. The Coffee Terminal Market Association of London
Robusta coffee
Lot size. 5 long tons.
Deposit per lot. £200.
Quotations. Pounds sterling and decimals per long ton.
Minimum fluctuation. £0·50 per long ton (£2·50 per lot).
Maximum fluctuation. No limit.
Trading positions. Up to 13 months ahead in: January, March, May, July, September, November.
Brokerage. Non-members, round-turn inclusive of fees £14. Market movement necessary to break even after commission £3·00.
Trading hours. Monday to Friday 1030 hours to close of 1220 hours call, 1430 hours to close of 1650 hours call.
Calls at 1030 hours, 1230 hours, 1430 hours, 1650 hours.

3. The Coffee Terminal Market Association of London
Arabica coffee
Lot size. 5865 kg.
Deposit per lot. $300.
Quotations. Dollars and cents per 50 kg.
Minimum fluctuation. 10 cents per 50 kg.
Maximum fluctuation. No limit.
Trading positions. Up to 13 months ahead in: February, April, June, August, October, December.
Brokerage. Non-members, round-turn £13.
Trading hours. Monday to Friday 1040 hours to close of 1230 hours call, 1430 hours to close of 1710 hours call.
Calls at 1040 hours, 1230 hours, 1440 hours and 1710 hours.

4. The United Terminal Sugar Market Association
Lot size. 50 long tons.
Deposit per lot. £250.
Quotations. Pounds sterling and decimals per long ton.
Minimum fluctuation. £0·05 per long ton (£2·50 per lot).
Maximum fluctuation. Trading is not permitted and contracts will not be registered for any business at £5 above or below the official quotations as established at the 1230 hours call. On the first day of the previous month, the spot or first delivery month shall be free of limit fluctuations.
Trading positions. Up to 15 months ahead in: March, May, August, October, December.
Brokerage. Non-members, round-turn inclusive of clearing fee £18. Market movement necessary to break even after commission £0·35.
Trading hours. Monday to Friday 1040 hours to close of 1230 hours call, 1430 hours to 1700 hours.
Calls at 1040 hours, 1230 hours, 1430 hours, 1530 hours, 1645 hours. A "kerb" market then continues until 2000 hours.

5. The Rubber Trade Association of London
Lot size. 5 metric tons per month (usually 5 tons monthly over three months).
Deposit per lot. £300.
Quotations. Pence and 20ths of pence per kg.
Minimum fluctuation. 0·05p per kg (£2·50 per 5 tons).
Maximum fluctuation. No maximum.
Trading positions. January/March, April/June, July/September, October/December (or any single month) up to 30 months ahead.
Trading hours. Monday to Friday 1100 hours to 1700 hours. Trading is permitted outside these times.

6. The London Corn Trade Association
Home-grown barley
Lot size. 100 long tons.
Deposit per lot. £200.
Quotations. Pounds sterling and decimals per long ton.
Minimum fluctuation. £0·025 per long ton.
Maximum fluctuation. No maximum but the Council shall have power to appoint a committee consisting of any number of members of the Association not being less than three, for the purpose of fixing and declaring daily quotations in such a manner and at such times as the Council may prescribe.
Trading positions. September, November, January, March and May.
Trading hours. Monday to Friday 1130 hours to 1330 hours, 1445 hours to 1615 hours.

7. The London Corn Trade Association
Home-grown wheat
Lot size. 100 long tons.
Deposit per lot. £200.
Quotations. In pounds sterling and decimals per long ton.
Minimum fluctuation. £0·025 per long ton.
Maximum fluctuation. No maximum but the Council shall have power to appoint a committee consisting of any number of members of the Association not being less than three, for the purpose of fixing and declaring daily quotations in such a manner and at such times as the Council may prescribe.
Trading positions. September, November, January, March and May.
Trading hours. Monday to Friday 1130 hours to 1300 hours, 1445 hours to 1615 hours.

8. The London Vegetable Oil Terminal Market Association
Soyabean oil
Lot size. 50 metric tons.
Deposit per lot. $1000.
Quotations. Dollars and cents per metric ton.
Minimum fluctuation. 25 cents per metric ton.
Maximum fluctuation. No limit.
Trading positions. Up to 13 months ahead in: January, March, May, July, September, November.
Brokerage. Non-members, round-turn £16.
Trading hours. Monday to Friday 1010 hours to 1240 hours, 1430 hours to 1710 hours.
Calls at 1010 hours, 1230 hours, 1430 hours and 1700 hours.

9. The London Vegetable Oil Terminal Market Association
Palm oil
Lot size. 50 metric tons.
Deposit per lot. £400.

Quotations. Pounds sterling and decimals per metric ton.
Minimum fluctuation. 25 pence per metric ton.
Maximum fluctuation. No limit.
Trading positions. Up to 13 months ahead in: February, April, June, August, October, December.
Brokerage. Non-members, round-turn £16.
Trading hours. Monday to Friday 1025 hours to 1250 hours, 1440 hours to 1720 hours.
Calls at 1025 hours, 1240 hours, 1440 hours and 1710 hours.

10. The London Wool Terminal Market Association
Dry-combed wooltops
Lot size. 2250 kg.
Deposit per lot. £250.
Quotations. Pence per kg.
Minimum fluctuation. 0·10 per kg.
Maximum fluctuation. No limit.
Trading positions. Up to 19 months ahead in: March, May, July, October, December.
Brokerage. Non-members, round-turn £16.
Trading hours. Monday to Friday for official calls 1115 to 1130 hours, 1515 to 1530 hours, 1615 to 1645 hours; Kerb 1645 hours to 1730 hours.

11. The London Metal Exchange
Copper wirebars
Lot size. 25 metric tons.
Deposit per lot. £1000.
Quotations. Pounds sterling and decimals per metric ton.
Minimum fluctuation. £0·50 per metric ton (£12·50 per lot).
Maximum fluctuation. No limit.
Trading positions. Cash for delivery on the following business day three months forward. It is also permitted to open positions for delivery on any date between cash and three months. Liquidation is by trading-in the relevant delivery date on any business day before that date.
Brokerage. Non-members, round-turn ½ per cent.
Trading hours. Morning: 1st ring 1200 hours to 1205 hours; 2nd ring 1235 hours to 1240 hours; Kerb 1305 hours to 1320 hours. Afternoon: 1st ring 1545 hours to 1550 hours; 2nd ring 1615 hours to 1620 hours; Kerb 1635 hours to 1710 hours.
Trading is permitted outside these times.

12. The London Metal Exchange
Tin
Lot size. 5 metric tons.
Deposit per lot. £500.

Quotations. Pounds sterling and decimals per metric ton.
Minimum fluctuation. £1 per metric ton (£5 per lot).
Maximum fluctuation. No limit.
Trading positions. Cash for delivery on the following business day three months forward. It is also permitted to open positions for delivery on any date between cash and three months. Liquidation is by trading-in the relevant delivery date on any business day before that date.
Brokerage. Non-members, round-turn ½ per cent.
Trading hours. Morning: 1st ring 1210 hours to 1215 hours; 2nd ring 1245 hours to 1250; Kerb 1305 hours to 1320 hours. Afternoon: 1st ring 1550 hours to 1555 hours; 2nd ring 1625 hours to 1630 hours; Kerb 1635 hours to 1710 hours. Trading is permitted outside these times.

13. The London Metal Exchange
Lead
Lot size. 25 metric tons.
Deposit per lot. £400.
Quotations. Pounds sterling and decimals per metric ton.
Minimum fluctuation. £0·25 per metric ton.
Maximum fluctuation. No limit.
Trading positions. Cash for delivery on the following business day three months forward. It is also permitted to open positions for delivery on any date between cash and three months. Liquidation is by trading-in the relevant delivery date on any business day before that date.
Brokerage. Non-members, round-turn 1 per cent.
Trading hours. Morning: 1st ring 1215 hours to 1220 hours; 2nd ring 1250 hours to 1255 hours; Kerb 1305 hours to 1320 hours. Afternoon: 1st ring 1540 hours to 1545 hours; 2nd ring 1605 hours to 1610 hours; Kerb 1635 hours to 1710 hours.
Trading is permitted outside these times.

14. The London Metal Exchange
Zinc
Lot size. 25 metric tons.
Deposit per lot. £400.
Quotations. Pounds sterling and decimals per metric ton.
Minimum fluctuation. £0·25 per metric ton.
Maximum fluctuation. No limit.
Trading positions. Cash for delivery on the following business day three months forward. It is also permitted to open positions for delivery on any date between cash and three months. Liquidation is by trading-in the relevant delivery date on any business day before that date.
Brokerage. Non-members, round-turn 1 per cent.
Trading hours. Morning: 1st ring 1220 hours to 1225 hours; 2nd ring 1255 hours to 1300 hours; Kerb 1305 hours to 1320 hours. Afternoon: 1st ring 1540 hours to

1545 hours; 2nd ring 1610 hours to 1615 hours; Kerb 1635 hours to 1710 hours.
Trading is permitted outside these times.

15. The London Metal Exchange
Silver
Lot size. 10,000 troy oz.
Deposit per lot. £1000.
Quotations. Pence and tenths of a penny per troy oz.
Minimum fluctuation. 0·10p per troy oz.
Maximum fluctuation. No limit.
Trading positions. Spot, three months, seven months forward.
Brokerage. Non-members, round-turn ½ per cent.
Trading hours. Morning: 1st ring 1205 hours to 1210 hours; 2nd ring 1300 hours
to 1305 hours; Kerb 1305 hours to 1320 hours. Afternoon: 1st ring 1555 hours
to 1600 hours; 2nd ring 1630 hours to 1635 hours; Kerb 1635 hours to 1710 hours.
Trading is permitted outside these times.

16. The London Bullion Market
Silver
Lot size. No minimum quantity. (Usual contract is 5000 fine oz.)
Quotations. Pence and tenths of a penny per troy ounce.
Minimum fluctuation. 0·10p per troy ounce.
Maximum fluctuation. No limit.
Trading positions. Spot, three, six and twelve months forward.
Brokerage. Non-members, round-turn ½ per cent.
Price fixing and trading hours. The official prices are fixed once daily (Monday
to Friday). The London brokers meet for fixing at 1215 hours. Orders for execu-
tion at the fixing time should therefore be received before this time. Dealing at
other times is subject to negotiation.

Index